Henry Fuseli
1741-1825

Tate Gallery 1975

Translation by Sarah Twohig

Exclusively distributed in France and Italy by Idea Books
24 rue du 4 Septembre, 75002 Paris and Via Cappuccio 21, 20123 Milan

ISBN 0 900874 87 2 cloth 0 900874 88 0 paper
Published by order of the Trustees 1975
for the exhibition of 19 February–31 March 1975
Copyright © 1975 The Tate Gallery
Designed and Published by the Tate Gallery Publications Department,
Millbank, London SW1P 4RG
Black-and-white blocks by Augustan Engravers Ltd, London
Printed in Great Britain by Balding & Mansell Ltd, Wisbech, Cambs.

Contents

Cover/Jacket
Garrick and Mrs Pritchard in Macbeth (1812)
(details of catalogue No.21)

Frontispiece
*Self-Portrait of the Artist c.*1777
(detail of catalogue No.2)

Foreword

We are delighted to have the opportunity to put on this exhibition of the work of Henry Fuseli, one of the most remarkable of that long line of painters who have made their home in this country. Unlike his compatriot Holbein or Van Dyck, he lived in England when English painting was at its peak – Reynolds, Gainsborough and Stubbs flourished when he arrived, Turner, Constable and Lawrence when he died. However, in many ways Blake was his closest colleague. Both artists made the human figure the vehicle of an imagination which, while intensely personal and realized with obsessive insistence, revealed much about the human mind and condition that remains fresh and exciting today – perhaps today more than ever.

A large share of the organisation of the exhibition has been undertaken by the Pro Helvetia Foundation, Zurich, and by the Hamburg Kunsthalle. We are extremely grateful for this and should like to thank especially the President of the Foundation Dr Willy Spühler, the Director Mr Luc Boissonas and Mrs Mirjam Lourié, formerly of the Foundation; also Dr Werner Hofmann, the Director, and Dr Georg Syamken of the Kunsthalle. Professor Gert Schiff, on whose compendious scholarship everything was based, made the original selection of paintings and drawings and contributed an important essay, together with the entries on all the works, to the catalogue. We are also grateful to His Excellency Dr A. Witnauer the Swiss Ambassador in London and to Mr Franz Birrer, Cultural Attaché, for their help in originating this project and to Dr Hans Lüthy, Director of the Swiss Institute of Art History, for the loan of the photographs.

As always, I am glad to acknowledge our debt to the lenders to the exhibition. In this case I must single out one among the many who have made the exhibition possible – the Kunsthaus, Zurich, and its Director, Dr René Wehrli, who have lent seventy works, a third of the whole show.

The exhibition has been shown in Hamburg and, after the Tate, will go on to the Petit Palais in Paris.

Norman Reid, Director

Fuseli, Lucifer and the Medusa

Henry Fuseli is the forerunner of the many exiled artists and writers of the twentieth century who – like Kandinsky, Picasso and Joyce – have never quite assimilated in their adopted domicile. It is even possible that they drew their revolutionary strength from this constant awareness of being the outsider. Fuseli lost his mother when he was an adolescent and his subsequent inability to feel he belonged anywhere may well be due to this. In old age he remarked: 'I always think in the language in which I write, and it is a matter of indifference to me whether it be in English, French or Italian; I know each equally well; but if I wish to express myself with power, it must be in German'. And the German he spoke throughout his life was the strong dialect of his native Zurich.

In 1763, aged 22, Fuseli left Switzerland. He was to return to his native country only once more, for a six-month stay in 1778. He soon gained a position of considerable importance in the English art world and was far more concerned than the majority of exiles to assimilate himself in English society. Yet the English always regarded him as 'teutonic'; this was not altogether untrue, for to the end of his life he remained faithful to the formative influences of his upbringing in Zurich.

In the middle of the eighteenth century Zurich was the intellectual capital of the German speaking countries of Europe. This was largely due to the influence of two native scholars Johann Jakob Bodmer and Johann Jakob Breitinger who also taught Fuseli at the Zurich Collegium Humanitatis for a time. Under Breitinger's guidance he became an enthusiastic classical philologist, while Bodmer introduced him to Homer, the Nibelungenlied, Dante, Shakespeare and Milton, from whom he was later to draw the main themes for his painting. He also adopted certain ideas from Bodmer's and Breitinger's aesthetic system that were to have a decisive impact on his art. Firstly, the dictum 'ut pictura poesis' according to which painting and poetry have the same aim, though they employ different means to achieve it. Secondly, an awareness of the allegorical character of all mythologies and the fact that they stem from the poetic 'image' as the expression of all fundamental human experience.

The atmosphere in the family home was both stimulating and restricting. His father was a much-travelled portrait painter and writer on art, an admirer of Winckelmann and Mengs. Hence the boy found himself surrounded by numerous drawings and engravings by sixteenth-century Swiss mannerists, which satisfied his precocious artistic talent; he also learned something about the emerging cult of the antique centred round Rome. Yet his autocratic father would hear nothing of his artistic inclination and decided he should become a Zwinglian minister. So the young Fuseli studied theology, began preaching and devoted himself generally to a wide variety of humanist studies. But as time went on he became more and more disillusioned. Things were brought to a head when, together with Lavater – the future physiognomist – and two other young theologians, he launched a public attack on a corrupt magistrate as a result of which they all had to leave the country. One consequence of this incident was that Fuseli began to doubt whether a just and reasonable form of government was a feasible reality at all.

In 1764 he went to London, where he soon found himself drawn to the richly varied literary and social activities it offered and decided to forsake theology. All that he retained from his theological training was a purely formal respect for Christianity and a vestige of Puritanism that was strangely at odds with his approach to art. The turning point in his intellectual development was undoubtedly his confrontation with Rousseau, as a result of which he finally lost all faith in the possibility of a reconciliation between the individual and society. He adopted Rousseau's conviction that art is the product of an irrevocably corrupt civilisation and came to the conclusion – astonishing at the time – that art and morality do not share the same aims at all. Yet Fuseli's aesthetic immoralism was also combined with a marked cultural elitism; he wanted to see education reserved exclusively for the highly gifted. It therefore seems not inappropriate that his own eccentric, at times esoteric, art should only have been appreciated by a small circle of intellectuals.

From this time on he devoted all his energies to painting. In 1770 he went to Rome to train as a painter. There he experienced his final disillusionment. Winckelmann's canon of beauty, his too harmonious view of antiquity and his condemnation of Michelangelo were powerless in the face of Fuseli's vehement emotional reaction to the Roman antiquities and the Sistine Chapel. Michelangelo's titanic figures, especially the plunging and floating figures in the 'Last Judgement' and the crouching 'Ancestors of Christ' sunk in thought, determined Fuseli's approach to the human body for the rest of his career. He fused these impressions with the flat compositional principles of neo-Attic and Roman relief sculpture. He was also to some extent influenced by Mannerism; hence he adopted Parmigianino's elegant though unnaturally elongated bodies, in particular for the female figure. He was also struck by Rosso's and Bandinelli's unreal, ghostly atmosphere, and Cambiaso's simplified, angular stylisation. He did not devote much time to life drawing, and for this reason his figures have a somewhat stereotyped quality. But he was by no means unskilled at making studies from nature, as can be seen from his many superb portraits and the few monumental landscape drawings of the south coast of England (Nos.201, 202, 205, 206).

In this way Fuseli developed a style which, once formed, remained essentially unchanged for the rest of his life apart from a few minor refinements. It is a style in which the human figure is the sole vehicle of expression: architecture plays almost no part in it. Space is largely defined by means of the broad gestures and strenuous movements of the figures behind whom it generally recedes into total darkness. In the interest of what he called 'poetic timelessness' costume and decor are not restricted to any specific historical period. Similarly, any individual characterisation is suppressed to emphasise the universally human quality. This was why Fuseli was so hesitant to create character portraits for Lavater's *Physiognomic Fragments*. His use of colour, which he later said he had courted all his life as a despairing lover courts a disdainful mistress, gives his figures the appearance of painted statues. He tended to juxtapose pale, slightly faded colours with bright areas of local colour, producing in his most successful paintings a shimmering silvery effect. Only in the last 15 years of his life when his drawing technique had achieved an almost ethereal, transparent quality did his painting technique become freer and his brushstrokes broader and more daring. The purple and cream tones he sometimes employed even remind one at a distance of Tintoretto. During his eight years in Rome he depicted scenes from Homer, the Greek tragedies, Dante and Shakespeare in this style, expressing his violent and tragic outlook on life. Pathos and bizarre effects are often combined in the most unexpected ways. Fuseli was without exaggeration the most original and progressive of all the artists working in Rome at the time, especially with regard to the high degree of abstraction in his forms as well as in his brilliant choice of themes and the subjective emotional energy he poured into his compositions. He duly became the central figure of an international circle of artists which included the Scandinavians Sergel and Abildgaard, the Scotsmen John and Alexander Runciman and John Brown, and the Englishmen Banks, Romney and Northcote.

By the time he returned to London in 1779 after his disappointing return visit to Zurich he was already famous. With Lavater's help, both Goethe and Herder had become staunch admirers of his work and the literary 'Sturm und Drang' movement recognised him as the artist who emulated their own aims in visual terms. Fuseli then set about introducing historical painting to England. Regardless of how we may view this now obsolete genre or, for that matter, Fuseli's own artistic merits, he was nevertheless the artist who considerably helped the introduction in to English art of monumental representations of scenes from literature, mythology and history.

At this point in his career Fuseli drew his subject matter primarily from Shakespeare. He was one of the initiators of Boydell's 'Shakespeare Gallery', an extensive undertaking in which every noteworthy English painter was involved. The aim was to set up a permanent exhibition of paintings of scenes from Shakespeare, of which engravings were then to be circulated abroad. Fuseli's contributions (e.g. No.28) were the most imaginative of all.[1]

The following paragraph from an essay by Giulio Carlo Argan sheds a good deal of light on Fuseli's attitude to Shakespeare:

Shakespeare's Mannerism lies in the fact that he is both actor and playwright; even more so in that he believes man's fate is to be an actor reciting a play written by an unseen hand without any time to rehearse . . . The actor moving across the stage is already in another dimension. It alters his bearing, gives his movements an unnatural emphasis and makes his voice resound unnaturally. It is precisely this artificiality that excludes him from nature. He stands alone in front of the dark crowded auditorium in the same way that man in Kierkegaard's vision stands alone before God. His only authentic existence is therefore the ritual of make-belief . . . What Fuseli really discovered in Shakespeare, apart from his immense dramatic variety, was the mysterious, secretive, orphic nature of the theatre.

Further on he continues:

Emotion has nothing pathetic or moving about it for Fuseli. He sees it in a purely moral light . . . it does not occur naturally in his works, but is to a certain extent artificial, like the emotional outbursts of the mad or the possessed. Fuseli found in Shakespeare the most suitable themes for his rebellious, failing morality.[2]

This last comment leads us directly to Fuseli's interpretations of scenes from Milton. The current exhibition in fact brings together twenty-one works connected with the 'Milton Gallery', the heroic task he undertook to carry out without the help of any of the other artists who had collaborated with him on the 'Shakespeare Gallery'. When looking at these works we should bear in mind that the real hero of Fuseli's illustrations to *Paradise*

Lost is Satan himself. Fuseli depicts him more frequently and highlights him more dramatically than any other figure, though carefully avoiding any suggestion of the popular contemporary interpretations of Satan as the bringer of light. A frustrated rebel and a pessimistic philosopher of history, Fuseli soon swung away from his initial support of the French Revolution to being a severe critic of it. Familiar as he was with the reality of human instincts at their most extreme – of which ample evidence is provided by his 'private' sketches and drawings – he can scarcely have believed in salvation through the senses as propounded with such passion by the theoretical hedonist, William Blake. Bound by his Puritan past Fuseli never achieved that total reversal of values undertaken by Blake and later Shelley in establishing Satan as an instrument of good. Despite his professed admiration in later life for Byron's complex heroes, he had little time for their predecessors, the 'beaux criminels' found in tales of horror. So what led him to make Satan the hero of his *Paradise Lost* illustrations?

The answer is to be found in one of the pictures of misery which the Archangel Michael places before Adam's eyes after the fall. In his depiction of 'The Lazar House' (No.102) Fuseli introduces a fleeing figure clearly demarcated from the other inmates who await their end lethargically. No such character appears in Milton's text; it is freely invented by Fuseli. He gazes accusingly at the spectre of death. But death is a divine law. The fleeing figure assumes the heroic stature of Satan. Can this not be interpreted as a repetition of Satan's fruitless rebellion on a human scale? Against the gloomy background of this place of despair it becomes evident that in Fuseli's eyes any opposition to suffering as the ruling force of the world is pointless. Yet the heroic splendour with which he invests both Satan and this fleeing figure makes it clear that he values the rebel – regardless of what he stands for – more highly than those who strike a compromise with the powers of this world or who acquiesce out of sheer indifference or apathy. Though his intentions were neither political, religious or philosophical, temperamentally Fuseli was definitely of the 'Devil's party' when he painted his 'Milton Gallery'.

Cat.102 Fuseli, *The Vision of the Lazar House*

In his series of water colour illustrations to *Paradise Lost* William Blake included a depiction of 'Adam Contemplating the Crucified Christ', as a prefiguration of the Redemption. We cannot know for sure whether Fuseli avoided this theme out of a Puritanical aversion to depicting the image of God, or simply because of his own lack of faith. Of the hopeful scenes shown by Michael to Adam he included only 'God's Covenant with Noah' (No.104).

Among the most intriguing of Fuseli's illustrations to Milton and Shakespeare are those based on themes from English fairy mythology. The fairies with their Queen Mab (No.96), that mischievous sprite, the 'Lubber Fiend' (No.105), and other even more mysterious spirits had only recently become the subject of serious study. Fuseli was one of the first artists to recognise the enormous visual potential of English folk superstition. In fact he had already drawn from this tradition when he painted ('The Nightmare' (No.159) and 'The Changeling' (No.167). In direct contrast to Winckelmann, who did not believe the Greek muses could ever have tolerated an evil spirit, Fuseli was fully aware of the demonic, ghostly undercurrents of classical mythology (Nos.71, 76, 77). In his illustrations to *A Midsummer Night's Dream*, Fuseli arbitrarily included the night-hags and their kith and kin, the changelings and incubi (Nos.24, 25). Equally idiosyncratic is his habit of dressing the fairies and witches in fashionable clothes (No.86) which he presumably intended as a criticism of contemporary society. From 1780 on there was a marked change in the outlook of

Cat.159 Fuseli, *The Nightmare*

intellectuals throughout Europe. The scepticism of the Enlightenment was by then a thing of the past, and it became fashionable to acknowledge the existence of even the most abstruse manifestations of the supernatural. Distinguished ladies from high society were among the first to form occult assemblies. Yet Fuseli, despite the fact that he painted so many ghost and witch scenes, never was an occultist. In marked contrast to Lavater he consistently denied any belief in miracles, or indeed in the existence of the supernatural at all. This attitude would also account for his practice of dressing the spirits in fashionable attire. With incredible irony he confronts the occult ladies with fairies and witches dressed in their own image. According to Xenophanes, the Ethiopians imagined their gods to be black-skinned and squat-nosed, and the Thracians imagined theirs to have blue eyes and red hair. Similarly, Fuseli's aim was to show that such spirits are nothing but figments of the misguided imagination of those who believed in them. In his light-hearted compositions he used these spirits as a means of social satire, though in his more sombre works they tend to personify the baser human instincts.

After the turn of the century Fuseli's work became increasingly influenced by his own scepticism and pessimism. He now interpreted the Siegfried saga – as he had earlier the murder of the king from *Hamlet* – (No.36) – as an allegory of the underworld attacking the sun or the destruction of a light principle by a dark, instinctual one. In this way he showed that the conflict between light and dark is intrinsic to the hero's character (cf. Schiff 1796 and Vol. I, p.316). Fuseli's interpretations of classical scenes alternate between pure tragedy and outright parody. An excellent example of the former is the drawing 'Achilles Grasps at the Shade of Patroclus' (No.66), in which the two figures are linked graphically to create a unified formal complex. Patroclus withdraws, Achilles, in his vain efforts to detain him, has fallen to the ground where he lies groping hopelessly. Fuseli depicts the nudes against a void; space is indicated summarily by the somewhat smaller proportions of the war chariot containing Hector's corpse. The bleak, timeless atmosphere of the drawing vividly evokes the isolation of the individual. By contrast, a drawing like 'The Daughters of Pandareus' (No.65), where the goddesses on Mount Olympus remind one of their caricatures in an Offenbach operetta, can only be interpreted as parody.

Fuseli frequently illustrated contemporary works of literature in a manner directly opposed to their overall mood or theme. It is somewhat difficult to see what can have drawn him to the poet William Cowper. He did, it is true, approve of Cowper's humanitarian and democratic convictions as can be seen from his paintings of 'The Negro Revenged' (No.133) and 'The Prison' (No.135). But Cowper – an unbalanced man living under constant threat of madness – also advocated a near-quietist way of life. His eulogy of the simple, natural country life is all too often interwoven with bigoted, moralistic overtones. Yet when Fuseli illustrated Cowper's diatribes against the corruption of urban civilisation he nevertheless managed to convey his own tolerance of everything the poet criticises. The women in these paintings, as Edmond Jaloux has pointed out, display 'a sovereign air of boredom, potential coquetry, forced comedy and involuntary melancholy'.[3] In this way Fuseli all but reversed the meaning of Cowper's parable of youth torn between virtue and vice (No.132).

Fuseli shared with the German Enlightenment poet Christoph Martin Wieland a profound scepticism, a worldly cosmopolitanism, an esoteric erudition and an artistic interest in the existence of ghosts and spirits that was spurned by contemporary philosophy. However, in his paintings he

Cat.66 Fuseli, *Achilles Grasps at the Shade of Patroclus*

transposed the mood of Wieland's romantic epic poem *Oberon* (1780) into a much darker key than that conveyed by the original (Nos.136–40). Barely a glimmer of the rococo lightness of Wieland's poetry emerges in Fuseli's sombre, tense illustrations. Even Byron was fascinated by the freedom with which Wieland handled the erotic. Proceeding from the maxim that 'reason and the senses are bound together' Wieland then decided to draw a veil of antique epicureanism over the unfathomed depths of the psyche. Fuseli, on the other hand, adopted a more direct approach. Hence he interpreted Huon's meeting with the Sultaness Almansaris (No.140) in terms of his own infatuation with the 'femme fatale'.

Fuseli worked consistently for many years to realise his conception of historical painting. To date virtually no research has been carried out on his relationship with those artists of his circle over whom he had such great influence. They included in the early years the Runciman brothers, Romney, Ottley, Prince Hoare, Banks and Northcote, followed later by Opie, Lawrence, Singleton, Westall (fig.1), Hamilton, Howard, Harlow and the sculptor Henry Rossi (fig.2). A detailed examination and analysis of their works would reveal to what extent Fuseli's idiosyncratic style can be said to have given rise to a new school of painting; for it is beyond dispute that he created a specific type of historical painting that greatly influenced English art for two decades after his death. His relationships to Blake (fig.3) and Haydon (fig.4) are more fully documented. In each case contact was sparked off initially by the younger man's boundless admiration for Fuseli, a powerful source of inspiration to both. Fuseli was doubtless impressed by Blake's naïvely seraphic, apocalyptical art (No.139); but their friendship foundered on account of Fuseli's rejection of the mystic and prophetic bias of Blake's thought. Haydon's veneration eventually turned to hatred when Fuseli refused to support his struggle for public recognition of the Parthenon sculptures which had been brought to London by Lord Elgin shortly before. Furthermore, Haydon could not tolerate Fuseli's blasphemy and unconventional morality. In spite of this, Fuseli's influence pervades the work of both these artists.

Through his teaching at the Royal Academy Fuseli exercised considerable influence over English art in general. In 1800 he was appointed Professor of Painting and in 1804, under a new statute, he was also appointed to the post of Keeper. There is no evidence that he exploited this second office to achieve any personal ambitions. On the contrary, it would be truer to say that he neglected this administrative side of his post. As a teacher he was extremely popular with the students. Both West and Flaxman confirmed how much progress the students had made under his guidance in drawing from classical models. Finally, in his twelve much read, frequently reprinted lectures he postulated a theory of art which, while not entirely free from contradiction, nevertheless influenced aesthetic thinking in England for a long time.

Fuseli's system is largely indebted to classicist art theory. Like Reynolds he believed that all great works of art originate in the last analysis from precise observation of nature. 'Our ideas are the offspring of our senses' he writes in the spirit of Locke's sensualistic theory of knowledge. From this we can deduce the extent of his differences from Blake, who held that every creative artist could transcend the boundaries of the visible universe and behold Eternity. Fuseli is therefore strongly opposed to the Romantic conception of the artist as a freely creative Promethean being. He adhered to the classical theory of selection according to which the ideal form must be distilled out of countless individual parts of beauty scattered throughout

Cat.140 Fuseli, *Almansaris Visits Huon in Prison*

Fig.1 R. Westall, *The Birth of Sin*, engraved by J. P. Simon, 1794

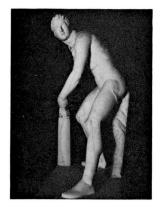

Fig.2 H. Rossi, *Cricketer*

Fig.3 William Blake, *The Lazar House* (Tate Gallery)

Fig.4 B. R. Haydon, *Dentatus*

nature. He stressed the superiority of drawing over painting, as also of the Roman and Florentine schools over their Venetian and Netherlandish counterparts, and even vilified the Mannerists with whom he had so much in common. He demanded that art reveal what he termed the timeless, universal essence. Though he upheld the supremacy and absolute pre-eminence of classical art, his classicism was very different from Winckel-mann's. Instead of 'noble simplicity and tranquil grandeur' Fuseli insisted that expression excelled mere beauty. He admired the vigour and original-ity of Rembrandt and Caravaggio, and in the last three lectures attri-buted greater importance than before to the study from nature. Given Fuseli's admiration for Michelangelo it seems astonishing that in old age he accused him of having neglected the modesty and variety of nature.

Yet he was fully aware of the new artistic developments. He described Turner as 'the only landscape painter of genius in all Europe', and he also foresaw the beginnings of bourgeois realism in the genre paintings of Wilkie. Many other statements in the lectures, for instance his rejection of all personal eccentricities and the way he condemned the depiction of cruel or frightening themes, are strongly at odds with his own work. One expla-nation for this would be that having had to sever so many of his own roots he needed the security of a rational doctrine endorsed by tradition. Fuseli's lectures still make fascinating reading, though this is due less to their classical structure than to their wealth of learning, astonishing insights and evocative description.

Finally, we come to the 'unofficial' side of Fuseli's personality that mani-fests itself primarily in his erotic works. One conspicuous feature in his figures has often been commented on but never fully explored: namely, his obsession with hair, in particular women's hair. This appears very early on in his career. Even in the 'Jugendalbum' (Youth Album) in the Zurich Kunsthaus, containing almost 300 drawings executed between the ages of ten and nineteen, there is one extraordinarily precocious sketch entitled 'Adelheide' (Schiff 218). This depicts an imaginary medieval noble-woman to whom Fuseli has given a rococo gown and, as Antal has noted, 'a perverse face and coiffure'.[4] In portraits of the clairvoyant Magdalena Schweizer-Hess (No.176) whom he met in Zurich on his way back from Rome he lavished immense care on the piled up rococo hairstyle with its profusion of plaits and tousled curls. Similarly, in the portrait of Anna Landolt on the back of 'The Nightmare' (No.159), he lingers with loving detail over the mass of powdered hair and coquettishly lifted plait.

Cat.159v Fuseli, *Anna Landolt*

During the first ten years of his marriage (1790–1800) he drew many portraits of his wife. From these we can trace her gradual transition from the lovely young wife to a domineering virago, as well as the changing hair fashions of the time. Both Fuseli and his wife attached equal import-ance to hair. He himself had his prematurely grey hair set and powdered each morning, and Mrs Fuseli was similarly obsessed with this aspect of her appearance. Until about 1795 she wore a complicated style in which the bulk of the hair, after being dressed with pomade and powder, was combed up strand by strand and the ends crimped with curling tongs. The result resembled a fluted diadem or halo, shaped like a double moon descending in a mass of tight curls almost to the bridge of the nose (Nos.165, 177–9). This effect obviously could not be achieved without the padding provided by a toque, the peak of which surmounted the magnificent construction like a small obelisk. A number of stiffly pasted curls projected on either side of the toque and a catogan, or wide loop of smooth hair, was knotted at the nape of the neck. Fuseli was evidently fascinated by this particular

Cat.177 Fuseli, *Mrs Fuseli with her Hair in Large Rolls*

hairstyle as it reappears in his drawings of courtesans, for which his wife was often the model. In about 1794 the influence of French revolutionary fashions began to make itself felt in England. Hence we see Mrs Fuseli with her hair dressed 'à la grecque', followed by the 'Titus style' created by Talma when he appeared in Voltaire's *Brutus* in 1790. But the latter style soon struck her as too formless. By the following year the curls are piled up still higher and in more orderly array, with three long rolls of hair behind each ear (No.181). At the end of the 1790s she entrusted herself to a hairdresser who created an even more extravagent style for her. Once again the catogan and pasted curls feature prominently. As before, the middle part of the hair is combed up high, falling over the forehead in a cascade of tight curls, and the effect is completed by a series of longish rolls of hair framing each side of the face. Mrs Fuseli is wearing this style in the drawing in which she is seated before the fire facing the spectator with her counter portrait as a threatening Medusa in a relief medallion on the wall (No.182).

Cat.182 Fuseli, *Mrs Fuseli Seated in Front of the Fire*

Over the following ten years Fuseli executed hardly any straightforward portraits of his wife. Instead, he tended to use her as his inspiration for a wide variety of female types. In the fantasy portrait of a woman with enormous ostrich feathers and a phallic emblem on her armband (No.190) he combined the characteristics of courtesan, actress and cruel mistress. Although her features have become monumentalised and somewhat coarsened, we still recognise the face as being the one familiar from the previous decade. The woman shown in another drawing (No.189) warming herself by an open fire dressed in a négligé, is generally referred to as a courtesan. The model is once again Mrs Fuseli. Her hair has been crimped with the curling tongs, but is now cut short and tied back severely as if she had to all intents and purposes overcome her vanity. Beside her crouches a small fairy with the features of Mrs Fuseli as we know her from the early years of her marriage, symbolising the order and comfort she had originally brought her husband. The switch in the hand of the coarser figure seems to indicate that the artist's libido was in need of occasional stimulus.

Cat.190 Fuseli, *Half-length Figure of a Courtesan*

Between 1810 and 1825 Fuseli made no further portraits of his wife apart from copies of a number of earlier works. But his preoccupation with women's hair did not die. During this period he concentrated on two widely diverging types of portrait: on the one hand the very young girls of his acquaintance whom he depicts with the slightly melancholic tenderness of old age; and those other fantastic creatures who seem as unreal as their convoluted coiffures. It is in this second category that the inherently sexual content of Fuseli's art makes itself most evident.

When he was over eighty he depicted one of his sheltered young female acquaintances, subsequently 'Mrs Otway Cave' (No.166), as a 'femme fatale' with a bizarre feather decoration in her hair, making her look far older than her years. Antal refers to the 'sensuous expressionist flavour' of this portrait, 'reminiscent of his drawings of courtesans. This treatment, so astonishing in a portrait, makes Goya's likeness of Queen Caroline seem objective and Girodet's portrait caricature of Mademoiselle Lange as Danaë seem naive'.[5]

Fuseli painted many unidentified female portraits representing real or imaginary mistresses. In these he evolved hair creations resembling nests, bells or upturned crowns of flowers. One figure, based on the kneeling woman in Raphael's 'Transfiguration', introduces us to a new, lascivious female type with a hooked nose and ringlets reaching down to her eyebrows, the rest of her hair being done in long plaits which part in the centre to reveal

Cat.198 Fuseli, *A Seated Woman with
an Extremely Eccentric Hairstyle*

her scalp (No.195). A frenzied swirl of vineleaves now weaves its way through the work of art created by the curling tongs, which is frequently pierced by a phallic arrow. Examples of this are the 'Half-length Figures of Two Promenading Women' (No.194) or the figure seen from the back whose egg-shaped head is shaved bare apart from a few tufts at the temples and the broad band of gleaming black hair fastened above the chignon with a mother-of-pearl comb (No.198).

If we are to attempt a closer understanding of these observations within the short space of this introduction, we must summarise briefly the findings of recent post-Freudian research into the phenomenon of fetishism. The following statements may at first seem strange to those who are unfamiliar with psychoanalytical theory; they are, however, based on phenomena clearly discernible in the mythologies of primitive peoples and highly developed civilisations alike, which psychoanalytical practice has confirmed operate equally strongly in the subconscious of modern man. Hair in its psycho-sexual significance is a fetish and fetishism is based on the illusion that all life-giving, life-preserving energy derives from the mother, whom the male child imagines as endowed with a phallus.[6] The fetish is an attempt to deny the woman's lack of a penis and the resulting male castration anxiety. The ambiguous character of Fuseli's female hair creations has been described above. It manifests itself even in those portraits of his wife executed in the first years of their marriage, where her coiffure combines the phallic obelisk-shaped toque with the extremely feminine flowing catogan. Later he even includes such obvious symbols as a bell or a nest pierced by an arrow. In drawings such as No.198 the phallic emphasis is counteracted by the shaven areas symbolising castration. Thus the artist while depicting a woman as his love object, gives her a penis and castrates her. This would seem to indicate an unresolved conflict between the desire for submission and aggression. Both presuppose a deep-rooted fear of the sexual partner. Aggression stems from the shock experienced by the baby when the mother's breast is withdrawn (object-loss), the final dissolution of its assumed oneness with the mother's body. As a result of this first experience of fear some men develop feelings of insecurity, mistrust and, as a reaction, even hatred towards women. It may even be the source of the fear of death.

The desire for submission is rooted in the child's defence against the fear of castration. The male child is profoundly disturbed by the discovery that his mother has no penis and feels threatened by a similar loss. Once again his trust in his mother as the protective, life-preserving force is shattered. The promise of unconditional love seems to be contradicted by the fearful threat of castration. The adult masochist yields anxiously to this threat. But the phallic fantasies he creates about the dominant woman to whom he subjects himself are an instance of projective identification by which he seeks to ensure the integrity of his own body. What he really desires is to return to the original protection of the womb.

This ambivalence can be seen in many of Fuseli's works. There is for instance in the Staatliche Kunstsammlungen, Dresden, a curious drawing 'Female Cruelty' (fig.5). The composition centres on the relationship between a man trapped in a well, of whom nothing is visible but a hand reaching for help, and a courtesan who mockingly holds her plait – his fetish – towards him as though he might be able to pull himself up on it. The scene illustrates the suffering and the piquant fascination of bondage, the confused mixture of fear and lust inherent in such relationships. However, since all creations of the unconscious have a multiple function, the well can also be identified as the womb, the plait as the severed umbilical

Fig.5 Fuseli, *Female Cruelty*

cord; the drawing then symbolises the unconscious desire to return to the womb. In direct contrast, man the avenger appears at the top of the drawing. He is totally unmoved by the pleas of the woman he is determined to kill.

Depictions of male surrender to female cruelty occur so frequently in Fuseli's work that they almost constitute his most personal form of expression; Julia and Pompeius, Queen Margaret and York (No.46), Brunhild and Gunther (No.142), Kriemhild and Hagen (No.147), Milton's Eva, Wieland's Almansaris and Huon (No.140), the Erinyes pursuing Orestes (No.74) or Alcmaeon (No.61). Especially interesting in this context is the wash drawing 'Dalila Visits Samson in the Prison at Gaza' (No.106). In the biblical story it is precisely the loss of his hair as the source of his strength that emasculates the hero. The scene in Milton's *Samson Agonistes* on which the drawing is based is perhaps the most violent depiction of the hatred between the sexes in literature before Strindberg. Delilah showers the imprisoned Samson with a torrent of hatred and scorn; Fuseli brings out the contrast between his clean-shaven head and her elegant, Empire-style coiffure. Just how deeply this desire for surrender permeated Fuseli's personality can be seen in the allegory depicting his artistic vocation (No.9): even painting is personified as a cruel female task-mistress. From an art-historical point of view it is interesting that it was Fuseli, not Gustave Moreau or Aubrey Beardsley, who introduced this theme into painting.

Aggression towards women is also implicit in 'The Nightmare' (No.159), arguably Fuseli's most famous painting. According to Janson the first version, executed in 1781, was inspired by his frustrated passion for Lavater's niece Anna Landolt. Tormented by unfulfilled desire he sent to his lost love the incubus as the embodiment of his longing, jealousy and resentment.[7] In some later works he depicted two lesbians disturbed by the intrusion of nightmares (Nos.160, 168). In each case only one of the languorous figures starts with fright when the incubus gallops through the window on his nightmare. Traces of his earlier jealousy are combined here with another form of resentment. A man's fantasies about sexual relationships between women are invariably the expression of his own repressed homosexuality. Hence the intrusion of the incubus would mean: Why should they be allowed to do what is forbidden to me? Interestingly, in a painting executed during his last creative period, Fuseli depicts two women sleeping peacefully in each other's arms visited on this occasion by a good-natured dream fairy.[8] (fig.6). In a series of drawings made during his Roman period Fuseli portrayed a man between a cruel and a loving mistress, as if caught between the conflicting poles of his desires. The conflict is resolved in favour of the cruel mistress.[9] While flirting with a coquette in Zurich on his way back from Italy, Fuseli met the woman he was to love more passionately than any other. Yet instead of pursuing the marriage he so desired with Anna Landolt, he wrecked any chance of it by flirting with Magdalena Schweizer-Hess who was safely married. A deep-rooted fear of committing himself always caused him to shrink back from the reality of a fulfilled relationship with a woman who was his equal. Sophia Rawlins, whom he married in 1788 when he was nearly 50, doubtless appealed to him on account of her youthfulness, but she was both intellectually and socially his inferior. To judge from contemporary reports she learned to play her role as the wife of a prominent man whenever they had to appear in society; in private she was reputed to be argumentative, vulgar and tyrannical, at least towards servants. In the portraits dating from the early years of their marriage she is presented as an extremely attractive

Cat.106 Fuseli, *Dalila Visits Samson in the Prison at Gaza*

Fig.6 Fuseli, *Queen Mab Visits Two Sleeping Women* (Edouard M. Sandoz)

Fig.7 Fuseli, *Symplegma; A Man with Three Women* (Victoria & Albert Museum)

Cat.155 Fuseli, *Undine Comes to the Fisherman's Hut*

Cat.67 Fuseli, *Achilles Sacrifices his Hair on Patroclus' Funeral Pyre*

young woman; yet even there a hint of obstinacy is apparent in her expression. Later on, in portraits like that done on 8 October 1796 (No.181) or in the heroically stylised drawing (No.190), her eyes have become domineering, cold, even cruel. In the absence of any detailed biographical information, the most we can hope to deduce about the Fuseli marriage is from studying his pictures. Mrs Fuseli's obsession with hair and fashion undoubtedly contributed to the attraction she held for her husband. In some of his mythological scenes the woman who dominates and destroys the man clearly bears Mrs Fuseli's features. This seems to indicate a feeling of subordination against which he retaliated by depicting her in other drawings as a courtesan; by degrading her in this way he possibly wanted to persuade himself he did not need her. On the other hand, it may have been precisely her willingness to gratify her husband's fetishistic and other desires that ensured the stability of their marriage. She may well have been both cruel mistress and loving wife to him.

There is a connection between Fuseli's portraits of his wife and those other works which reveal his unconscious fear and hatred of women. An example of this is the drawing mentioned previously in which he included a second portrait of her as a Medusa in a medallion on the wall (No.182). Many other instances can be cited. In No.147 the figure of Kriemhild, confronting Hagen with the severed head of Gunther in her hand, is based on the iconographic precedent of Perseus with the Medusa's head; she too has Mrs Fuseli's features. Freud interpreted the petrifying effect of the Medusa's head as the shock experienced by the male child at the sight of the 'multilated' female genital.[10] Among those of Fuseli's works which were not meant for publication are numerous drawings and paintings of courtesans sexually injuring or mutilating young boys. The study of Medea with the inscription 'Paidoleteira' – child-murderess – belongs in this category (No.197). Freud's idea that fear of castration replaces fear of death in the unconscious is also illustrated in several of Fuseli's later works. In his imaginary portrait of Mary Anne Lamb (No.193), a girl who had murdered her mother, the petrifying Gorgon has become a goddess of death in the guise of a maenad. One late drawing even includes a direct reference, with a characteristic touch of self-hate, to death as the ultimate fulfilment or release from masochistic craving (fig.7; Schiff 1620). The scene depicts a man clearly deriving great pleasure from the sadistic ministrations of three beautiful women. It is inscribed with a quotation from Aeschylus' *Prometheus*: 'In such wise may Love come upon mine enemies!' These words refer to the sons of Aigyptos who were murdered by their brides the Danaids on their wedding night.

In Fuseli's later works the Gorgon is contrasted with the nymph Undine (Nos.141, 155–158), with her fluctuating moods, wantonness and utter loyalty. Once again, woman is seen as the source of both pain and pleasure. Undine's artless curls dripping with water could not differ more from the bizarre coiffures of the 'femmes fatales'. Biographically, Undine is the exact image of the aristocratic young girls who filled the aging Fuseli with such melancholy tenderness. This prompts one to wonder whether the lascivious figure also had a counterpart in real life.

All contemporary accounts agree that Fuseli's last years were marked by an extremely regular and frugal way of life. With age he probably found increasing satisfaction in being able to gratify his obsessions in those works not intended for publication. Seen in these terms, the cult of hair amounted to the same thing as the subsequent sacrifice of it. One of his greatest drawings, 'Achilles Sacrifices his Hair on the Funeral Pyre of Patroclus' (No.67) can be interpreted in psychological terms as the sacrifice of primitive inclinations to the higher aims of civilisation.[11]

Assuming that Fuseli had been admitted to the ranks of the immortal, he would have appeared in the heavens after his death like the soul of Caesar in Roman popular belief[12] in the form of a 'stella crinita', or long-haired star (vulgo: comet).

[1] See T. S. R. Boase, 'Illustrations of Shakespeare's Plays in the Seventeenth and Eighteenth Centuries', in *Journal of the Warburg and Courtauld Institutes*, X, 1947.

[2] G. C. Argan, 'Fuseli, Shakespeare's Painter', in an edition of Shakespeare's Plays, ed. C. V. Lodovici (Einaudi, 1960); quoted by Mario Praz in *Il patto col serpente*, Mondadori, 1971, pp.18–19, note 1 (transl.).

[3] Edmond Jaloux, *Johann-Heinrich Füssli*, Montreux 1942, p.138.

[4] Frederick Antal, *Fuseli Studies*, London 1956, p.10.

[5] Ibid., p.163.

[6] See Warner Muensterberger, 'Der schöpferische Vorgang, seine Beziehungen zum Objektverlust und zum Fetischismus', in *Jahrbuch der Psychoanalyse*, vol.IV, 1967, and W. Muensterberger, 'Vom Ursprung des Todes, eine psychoanalytisch-ethnologische Studie zur Todesangst', in *Psyche*, vol.3, 1963.

[7] See Horst W. Janson 'Fuseli's Nightmare', in *Arts and Sciences*, II, Spring 1963, I.

[8] Schiff 1504.

[9] See Schiff I, pp.113–16.

[10] Sigmund Freud, *Collected Papers*, II, XX.

[11] See K. A. Menninger, 'Study of the Significance of Self-Mutilation', in *The Psychoanalytic Quarterly*, IV, 1935, p.462.

[12] Suetonius, *Iulius*, LXXXVIII.

28 **Titania's Awakening** [1785–9] (entry on p.63)

90 **The Creation of Eve** (1793) (entry on p.88)

117 **Dante and Virgil on the Ice of Cocytus** 1774 (entry on p.101)

124 **Percival Delivering Belisane from the Enchantment of Urma** (1783) (entry on p.105)

125 **Thor Battering the Midgard Serpent** [1790] (entry on p.105)

132 **Virtue Calling Youth from the Arms of Vice** [1806–7] (entry on p.108)

134 **Mad Kate** [1806–7] (entry on p.109)

163 A Nude Reclining and a Woman Playing the Piano [1799–1800] (entry on p.124)

A Captive

Just how explicitly must an artist express himself today to avoid accusations of being speculative or devious? Realism, the catch-phrase of the moment, is fatally suited to hinder or falsify the debate so long as it amounts to nothing but the most convenient way of making a straightforward pictorial statement which is then taken at face value. This approach totally overlooks the fact that disguise is a legitimate and frequently used artistic device. In 1888 Nietzsche wrote in *The Case of Wagner*: 'Would you believe it, as soon as the heroic mask is removed, every one of Wagner's heroines is so like Madame Bovary as to be almost indistinguishable! On the other hand Flaubert was perfectly at liberty to transfer his heroine to a Scandinavian or Carthaginian setting and then to offer her in mythological form to Wagner'. Behind any attempt to project the present into the past there lurks both the need for identification as well as the necessity for concealing it.

Something of this fusion of levels is contained in the Ossian cult (so popular in the late eighteenth and early nineteenth centuries). If we remove the 'heroic mask' we are left with fundamental human situations and ways of behaviour. The Colma, Comal, Colmala, Comala, or whatever names are used, provide only the pseudomythological justification, a mask behind which to escape from the present. The same applies to the 'Caprichos' and 'Proverbios' in which Goya, the most significant artist at the turn of the nineteenth century, resorted to artistic obscurity to avoid the suspicion of the censor. Caspar David Friedrich is another artist who distinguishes himself as a master of the ambiguous statement, though for totally different artistic and social reasons. Instead of using human protagonists, he makes familiar elements of the visible world into ciphers that can be interpreted in several different ways, thus posing many problems for the art historian.

Cat.65 Fuseli, *The Daughters of Pandareus*

Fig.8 Fuseli, *Britomart freeing Amoretta from the spell of Busirane* (Frankfurt, Goethe Museum)

With Fuseli, things are different again. He, too, is a complex artist, preferring the complicated to the simple, the curve to the straight line. He gives no clear-cut, straightforward answers. In fact, it is debatable whether he is giving us answers at all, or whether he is simply playing a masquerade with us, fooling us with a virtuoso psychological and artistic performance. Fuseli is a master of allusion, quotation and paraphrase which, together with his wide range of forms and themes, makes him an ideal subject for art historical probings. His very scholarliness surrounds his works like some rare esoteric mist, causing much perplexed shaking of heads. What are we to make of 'Meleager Implored by the Aetolians to Defend the City of Calydon' (Schiff 380) or 'The Daughters of Pandareus' (No.65)? What does 'Britomart Freeing Amoretta from the Spell of Busirane' (fig.8) mean to us? What, if anything, has this artist to say to us today?

Since all these questions reflect contemporary attitudes one begins to suspect that they are blindly trying to pinpoint a personality whose stature and significance can only be ascertained from the specific context of his own epoch. This objection is unjustified for two reasons; in the first place, it is not our prime concern to present Fuseli in a topical light; and secondly, it is not necessary to pose questions of a topical nature in order to come to terms with the fundamental problems of Fuseli's art. He himself gave much thought to these problems. He was also well aware of the fact that not all subject matter is accessible to everyone at all times. He acknowledged that the 'message' conveyed by a work of art cannot be universally valid and for this reason distinguished between three different classes of theme:

> Subjects are positive, negative, repulsive. The first are the proper materials, the voluntary servants of invention; to the second she gives interest and value; from the last she can escape only by the help of execution, for execution alone can palliate her defeat by the last. The Laocoon, the Hæmon and Antigone, the Niobe and her daughters, the death of Ananias, the Sacrifice at Lystra, Elymas struck blind, are positive subjects, speak their meaning with equal evidences to the scholar and the unlettered man, and excite the sympathy due to the calls of terror and pity with equal energy in every breast. St. Jerome presenting the translation of his Bible to the Infant Jesus, St. Peter at the feet of the Madonna receiving the thanksgivings of victorious Venice, with every other votive altar-piece, little interesting to humanity in general, owe the impression they make on us to the dexterous arrangement, the amorous or sublime enthusiasm of the artist; – but we lament to see invention waste its powers, and execution its skill, to excite our feelings for an action or event that receives its real interest from a motive which cannot be rendered intuitive; such as Alceste expiring, the legacy of Eudamidas, the cause of Demetrius's disorder. (Aphorism 239)

Fuseli himself deals with none of the themes he describes as 'positive'. On the other hand, he takes themes at random from classical mythology and history, from Christian art, and from literature – from the *Nibelungenlied*, Dante, Shakespeare, Milton and Wieland – regardless of whether he is aiming at an uneducated or an educated audience. And he was not content with this range of themes; he was also concerned with topics that could not be expressed adequately through the repertoire of traditional subject matter.

In a letter regarded by Schiff as 'a very important statement of Fuseli's artistic self-awareness', he quotes some of his ideas for compositions which he refers to as 'philosophical ideas made intuitive, or sentiments personified'. They include a depiction of a man seated in a reflective pose, at his feet the body of an apparently dead woman (fig.9). Anyone not knowing the title could take it for an illustration of Hamlet meditating over the corpse of Ophelia. (The formal scheme, vaguely reminiscent of a Pietà, is encountered, somewhat modified, in two other works depicting scenes of mourning, 'Lady Constance', No.29, and 'Ugolino', fig.10). Fuseli immediately removes any doubts, for his title informs us that the subject of the picture is 'Ezzelin and Meduna'. Well and good, but what precisely is happening? The figures' relationship one to another needs commentary. Fortunately, we possess documentary evidence of Fuseli's aims. He in fact invented both scene and characters. On returning from the Crusades, Ezzelin Bracciaferro, a fictive Duke of Ravenna, accused his wife of being unfaithful and killed her. In the early seventies Fuseli dealt with this theme in a drawing representing Meduna at the executioner's block with Ezzelin, visibly distressed, in the background (Schiff 416). To some extent the situation resembles the Othello-Desdemona conflict. The central idea of the picture, that of reflecting on an act of vengeance already committed, was conceived in February 1779 in Zurich, where Fuseli spent six months

Fig.9 Fuseli, *Ezzelin and Meduna* (London, Sir John Soane Museum)

Cat.29 Fuseli, *Lady Constance, Arthur, Salisbury*

Fig.10 *Ugolino and his Sons Starving to Death in the Tower*, line engraving by Moses Haughton after Fuseli (Zurich, Kunsthaus)

Fig.11 Fuseli, *Self-Portrait with Bodmer*
(Zurich, Kunsthaus)

Cat.2 Fuseli, *Self-Portrait*

on his way back from Rome to London. During this same period he also began the famous self-portrait with the aged Bodmer (fig.11). He actually completed both paintings back in London and sent them to Switzerland in 1781. So far no one has remarked on the similarity between the self-portrait and the brooding figure of Ezzelin, both in facial expression and general pose. An important link, with reference to Ezzelin's frontality, is contained in a self-portrait sketch dating from 1777 (No.2) in which the artist is characterised by the same attitude of forbidding self-questioning as Ezzelin. In consciously or sub-consciously portraying himself as Ezzelin, Fuseli was in fact slipping behind the mask of a fictive character of his own creation. And it was not by mere chance that the Ezzelin theme should have come to his mind again in Zurich. During his stay in his native city he had affairs of a partially passionate, partially sentimental nature with the Hess sisters and Anna Landolt – the 'Nanna' of his stormy love poems – all of which ended in failure and alienation. Apparently Anna's father opposed his daughter's marriage to Fuseli. It is possible that all these tensions found sublimated form in the painting of Ezzelin and Meduna, which almost seems to reflect Fuseli's own violent reaction to the disappointment he himself had experienced in real life; for it depicts the most extreme form of parting – the murder of the partner.

These suggested interpretations are intended to supplement the character portrayal that Gert Schiff, with great psychological perception, has deduced from the artist's erotic entanglements. He speaks of Fuseli's 'deep-rooted fear of commitment' that causes him to flee from any possible fulfilment through love. Schiff argues that Fuseli was *incapable* of 'giving himself completely to any one person or cause'. One might suggest that Fuseli's extraordinary vitality and ability as an artist is to be found precisely in this inability.

In May 1770 Fuseli arrived in Rome the final destination of his journey from London. During the next eight years he devoted himself to a wide variety of personal, antiquarian and art historical interests. In this essay we shall concentrate on one seemingly peripheral aspect which, for our present purposes, proves extremely informative. He and the sculptor Thomas Banks devised an artistic exercise, the object of which was to sketch figures round a series of five arbitrarily placed points indicating the position of head, hands and feet. This was a good deal more than the mere game it may seem at first glance. For the resulting figures naturally assumed poses involving difficult anatomical problems especially as regards foreshortening. Fuseli and Banks composed drawings of this kind round identical points and then compared the results (Schiff p.80).

The idea, in principle, is not new. In Villard de Honnecourt's pattern book for masons, dating from the thirteenth century, we find similar geometrical schemes in which the draughtsman merely had to fill in various different objects. Without knowing about Fuseli's versions, Moritz von Schwind[3] later constructed acrobatic figures over a given constellation of fifteen points. This procedure finally emerges again in the geometric art of the twentieth century, characterised by the combination of line and plane in every possible variation.

In Fuseli's case the two factors involved are a frame of reference determined by the points and an adaptable motif – the human figure – with which to fill this abstract system in any chosen way. As with the rules of any game, these two factors necessarily restrict the freedom of the player or draughtsman. But within the scope of this limitation, he is free to combine things just as he pleases. Anatomical invention is actually *freed* by being subjected to rules. Constraint and freedom are thus brought into a dialectical relationship. This leads to two things: firstly, the artist finds himself developing the most extraordinary and daring poses of which the human anatomy is capable. Utilising his knowledge of form, he begins to think in terms of processes. A second consequence of these purely technical aspects is that the theme – the human being – is split up into many variations which then become themes in their own right. Artistic invention can be said to proceed in a permanent knight's move. Resisting any attempt to prescribe its ultimate form, it aims instead to master every possible configuration within the area of play. It offers not one, but a whole spectrum of solutions. Seen in the light of the psychological findings already referred to, this means that Fuseli denies himself any possibility of fulfilment, that he rejects an exclusive commitment to any particular form. There is a good deal more to the five-point drawings than a mere virtuoso performance or exercise; they are a key factor throwing light on the most intimate aspects of Fuseli's life and its artistic expression in the erotic drawings. At the same time they provide the basis for an understanding of the other extreme of his art, namely his 'official' paintings. Both spheres are therefore interwoven.

An artist whose basic formula involves constructing the nude round five points is clearly performing a kind of ritual that can have painful, even torturous consequences. Fuseli's imagination immediately thematised these contortions, i.e. applied them to related iconographical prototypes. This is confirmed by some of his five-point drawings: 'A Captive' (fig. 12), a 'Man on St. Andrew's Cross' and 'Prometheus', the classical anarchist-martyr (No.78). What all these figures have in common is that they are firmly nailed to their instrument of torture. It requires no great effort to see a connexion between the five-point drawings and the general theme of the martyr or maltreated captive, a theme Fuseli frequently treated in official works. Then we remember that even as a precocious fifteen-year-old he had made a sketch of a captive (fig.13). And again, one thinks of the drawings of fettered men being roughly handled or sexually stimulated by several women. In these erotic drawings (Schiff 539–549, 1381, 1620, 1770, 1810, fig.7) the five-point system is used to show all the possible ways by which individuals can arouse and satisfy each other's sexual desires. The same insatiable instinct to exploit every combination and variation imaginable which caused him to reject specific, unequivocal solutions for the ambivalence of the five-point drawings, now dominates the relationship between the sexes. Fuseli deduces from his own inability to commit himself totally that hetero-sexual relationships cannot be subject to either moral norms or aesthetic rules. On the contrary, every possible variation should be explored. And where valid norms no longer apply, moral or aesthetic accusations of 'deviousness' automatically become irrelevant. Artistic and erotic experiences proceed à rebours, against the grain; this activity can be best described by the word 'perversio' used in its widest sense, namely overthrow, reversal, distortion and perversion. Sexual intercourse becomes an endless complex of 'ars combinatoria'. Here too, his fear of a genuine, fulfilled relationship (Schiff) prevents Fuseli from achieving his aim. In his erotic drawings his tendency to explore the endless variations of any formal idea, to split up and recombine elements in different ways, in short his restless awareness of the endless possibilities that exist, all point to one thing – his underlying masochism. Seen in this intimate context it becomes clear that Fuseli's freedom of expression is at the mercy of this compelling desire for variety, is in fact enslaved by it. Even debauchery must submit to ritual.

Fig.12 Fuseli, *A Captive*

Cat.78 Fuseli, *Prometheus*

Fig.13 Fuseli, *A Captive*

Fig.7 Fuseli, *Symplegma; A Man with Three Women* (London, Victoria and Albert Museum)

Cat.60 Fuseli, *The Blinded Polyphemus*

Fig.14 William Blake, *Captive Giant*

Cat.54 Fuseli, *Dido on the Funeral Pyre*

Fig.15 Fuseli, *Unidentified Scene*
(London, British Museum)

The way these drawings subtly unite actual physical facts with a kind of anatomical acrobatics, and aggressor and victim are apparently linked in 'play', means that they conjure up precisely the ambivalent core of experience composed of the extremes of triumph and despair. This dichotomy is found throughout Fuseli's work in the two role-playing figures of the long-suffering victim and the superman.

It therefore seems justifiable to suspect that this wide range of variations in fact conceals Fuseli's own 'philosophical ideas made intuitive, or sentiments personified'. Fuseli uses countless heroes from mythology or literature to symbolise the fundamental tragic elements of human behaviour: jealousy and faithlessness, evil abuse and violence, mental confusion and the longing for salvation, the desire for power and the instinct for submission. These 'personified sentiments' find their supreme embodiment in the figure of 'Satan' as he emerges in all his sovereignty from Milton's verse[4] and this in turn reflects upon the two extreme concepts of Fuseli's repertoire; on the one hand the angrily insurgent form of the peerless man of action, contemptuous of all norms, and on the other, the 'superman' thrown back into introversion, forced to atone, rather like 'Polyphemus' (No.60) an image borrowed quite logically by Fuseli from Blake's 'Orc' (fig.14), the bound giant 'his face buried in acceptance of defeat'[5]. Satan, is both the captive of his own revolt and the ultimate result of the 'perversio' i.e. total overthrow or downfall.

Such interpretations can also be seen in relation to the five-point system. The latter, interpreted as a psychological pattern symbolising the perpetual tension and conflict between human beings, is variously filled (i.e. made concrete, graphic) by mythological or literary protagonists. On one level they can be read as variations on specific human themes. On the other hand such protagonists as Prometheus and Siegfried, Lady Macbeth and Melusine provide the 'heroic mask'; underneath the mask of virtue and culture lurk the prototypes of the brutal power-seeker, the disturbed and the insane, the failed outsider and the femme fatale.

The general rule that each of these categories – for example, the femme fatale – can be applied to many characters (Lady Macbeth, Brunhild, Salome) is also reversible. Not only can 'sentiments personified' be applied to a variety of personifications; a single formal pattern can also carry a large number of meanings. The same figure seen from behind appears in one instance as Hephaestus chaining Prometheus to the rock (No.73), while on another occasion it is used for the figure of Anubis proclaiming the 'Fertility of Egypt' (Schiff 974). Similarly, the pose of the 'Bard' (Schiff 1037) resembles that of 'Satan Calling Beelzebub'. Again, one could cite the similarity between 'Dido on the Funeral Pyre' (No.54), a drawing (fig.15) and the dead 'Sarpedon' (No.57). In each case the intensity of emotion and the significance of the figures in the composition are determined by the relevant literary context. Once again we encounter the phenomenon of variation, though the symptoms differ somewhat. The question here is no longer how many symbols can be related to a specific meaning, but how many meanings can be absorbed by a constant symbol. For example, long before Fuseli could have known the Barberini faun he drew seated men with splayed legs, such as Hadlaub dreaming (fig.16), a sleeping fool (Schiff 231) and a drunken cleric (fig.17) whose drinking partner, incidentally, prefigures a pose brought to classical perfection during the Roman period (Schiff 560, 601). Later on he used this pose to depict states other than sheer animal passivity. In one instance it appears under the rubric of coarse sensuality ('Falstaff in the Washing Basket',

Schiff 883), while on another occasion it turns up as a symbol of cautious expectation (Bottom in 'Titania Awakes', No.28). In the figure of the despairing 'Polyphemus' (No.60) the legs are stiff, while in 'Prometheus' (No.73) they are splayed open for the obscene ritual of pain. Falstaff and Prometheus represent the two extremes of these 'variations on a theme'. Many other examples can be found in Fuseli's work. This would seem to prove that he even treated his formal constants centrifugally, that he liked to invest his standard formulae with as many levels of meaning and intensity as possible. The prototype, whether drawn from classical models or freely invented, becomes a convenient, highly adaptable 'quotation'. As before, the possible variations on a theme become a substitute for the theme itself.

Fig.16 Fuseli, *Hadlaub Dreaming* (Zurich, Kunsthaus)

Starting with the simple, homogeneous forms of the five-point drawings we have tried to trace Fuseli's basic method of composition. Logically, this brings us to consider those more complex compositions containing a larger number of figures. In a sense, though, we hinted at the connexion already when we noted that the subsidiary figures are just as important as the chief protagonists in establishing the specific context of the scene. It is they, in fact, who largely create the particular situation and make it explicit.

Fuseli was aware of the 'many different levels' of expression, which he defined as follows:

> the palpitation of Hamlet cannot degenerate into vulgar fright. . . a lovely child taking refuge in the bosom of a lovely mother is an idea of nature, and pleasing in a lowly or domestic subject; but amidst the terrors of martyrdom, it is a shred tacked to a purple robe. (Aphorism 98)

Fig.17 Fuseli, *Two Drunken Clerics* (Weimar Staatliche Kunstsammlungen)

The analogy is reminiscent of the collage technique.

Fuseli's theses and recommendations hardly ever correspond to his own practice. An example of the way he openly contradicted himself is demonstrated by his attempts to heighten (i.e. ennoble) or debase a theme. An example of the former would be his depiction of blind Polyphemus where he succeeds in 'creating a figure of existential or animal tragedy out of a bloodthirsty monster' (Schiff p.311). And then there is the depiction of the imprisoned Malvolio invested with the dignity of Job (Schiff 1264). Examples of the opposite, debasing, tendency include the quartet of goddesses gazing down from Olympus on Pandareus and his daughters (No.65). 'Dogmatic Artemis, coquettish Aphrodite, curious Athena and the portly matron Hera appear for the first time cynically divested of their majesty' (Schiff, p.186). Fuseli's intention in juxtaposing the earthly and the Olympic spheres in this way was presumably to paraphrase the very linking of the different 'modi' he had spurned as a theorist in his analogy of the shred and the purple robe. Similarly, the drawing showing a voyeuristic Brunhild watching Gunther suspended from the ceiling (No.142) has something of the mood of ironical ambiguity encountered subsequently in Rops and Beardsley. (In this context a comparison can be made between Fuseli's 'Strife of the Queens', Schiff 1798, and Rops' watercolour 'L' Attrapade' in the Musées-Royaux, Brussels).

Cat.142 Fuseli, *Brunhild Watching Gunther Suspended from the Ceiling*

Fuseli's habit of quoting, adapting and paraphrasing a wide range of gestures and pathos formulas drawn from various sources, some obscure, some familiar, often displays its inherent limitations. We find ourselves confronted by an artist whose power to distil and amalgamate spans the entire breadth of classical and anti-classical (i.e. mannerist) forms, but who sometimes fails to combine elements of the most disparate origins into a homogeneous whole. The result is often a collage of quotations that can easily be divided up into its separate elements and reassembled in a slightly different way. Once again, we are reminded of the process of the five-point drawings.

Collages of quotations. With his work characterised by a concept rated highly in twentieth-century art, even counted among its innovations, Fuseli can be seen in the light of a precursor. Can he in fact be described as such, or was he simply an isolated case whose work heralds some of the features of modern art? As a classically orientated theorist he rejected the notion of collage. As a painter, he practised it, though scarcely with the romantic aim – taken up later by the Surrealists – of experimenting with what Novalis called 'amusing medleys'. If Fuseli can be said to mark the beginning of a line of compilers leading up to, for example, Max Ernst's collage 'novels', it completely contradicts his declared aim of creating homogeneous compositions. If anything, judged by his own aims he represents the end of a line, which lends him something of a tragic stature. For the last time the entire cultural wealth of the Mediterranean tradition is proclaimed, and it transpires that its encyclopaedic range is totally interchangeable. Hence the temptation to find more and more new combinations. If everything can be associated with everything else, there can be no unique combinations. The fact that everything is dispensable argues that there can be no ultimate cohesion.

Fuseli once noted: 'He who conceives the given point of a subject in many different ways, conceives it not at all'. (Aphorism 73). Paradoxically, this notion applies often to his own work. For instance, the theme of 'Samuel Appearing to Saul with the Witch of Endor' (No.108, fig.19) exists in two versions. In one the witch extends her arms in a Raphaelesque pose, whereas in the other version she turns to face the spectator. Yet in both instances she acts as mediator between Samuel and Saul. Without the rhetorical link the confrontation would presumably have seemed harsher and more abrupt. These compositions should really be classed as phenomena aiming at provoking a strong emotional reaction of fear and faintness. Is the figure of Saul intended as a depiction of 'sentiments personified', in other words, distanced behind the mask of a classical quotation? This clearly begs the question, but a comparison with Goya's treatment of the 'Tantalus' theme in the 'Caprichos' (fig.18), makes it apparent that confusion is the price Fuseli has to pay for his extensive knowledge of form. Goya probably compiled his compositions from various sources too. The figure of Tantalus wringing his hands in despair is reminiscent of the pathos formulae used to depict lamentation and burial scenes, and the woman possibly derives from the same antique source that Fuseli used for the figure of Saul.[6] The decisive fact is that Goya suggests a combination of horror and lust by means of formal discord, whereas Fuseli attempts to orchestrate the scene by means of harmony. Which brings us back to the starting-point of our considerations. Fuseli's 'wealth' – a deliberately exaggerated formulation – the vast fund of variations he can draw on, eventually becomes a hindrance. He knows too much and is too skilful. He is, in short, the prisoner of his own abilities. His fascinating sophistication and gift for composition mar the originality of his works. Reynolds, who recommended Fuseli to become a painter in the first place, discussed this very problem in his Third Discourse (1770):

> And, indeed, I cannot help suspecting, that in this instance the Ancients had an easier task than the Moderns. They had, probably, little or nothing to unlearn, as their manners were nearly approaching to this desirable simplicity; while the modern Artist, before he can see the truth of things, is obliged to remove a veil, with which the fashion of the times has thought proper to cover her.

Cat.108 Fuseli, *Samuel Appears to Saul, in the Presence of the Witch of Endor*

Fig.18 Goya, *Tantalus*

Fig.19 Fuseli, *Samuel Appears to Saul* (Zurich, Kunsthaus)

What moved Fuseli in 1805 to copy a Mongolian funerary statue illustrated
in a contemporary travel account (Schiff 1169)? Was he possibly following
Reynolds' advice to 'unlearn'? Did he perhaps see the stiff frontality of the
pose as a way of freeing himself from his highly sophisticated forms and
returning to more basic ones again? Clearly, surmisals of this nature must
be purely speculative. However, we know that frontality plays a considerable role in Fuseli's repertoire. Schiff has shown that one of his greatest
inventions, 'Silence' (No.98), was in fact inspired by Blake. It is the climax
of his introverted figures, which as a whole developed independently of
Blake. In this context Novalis' comments on the 'great misery' of existence
seem particularly appropriate: 'Devoid of inclination, man stands alone
like a perishable force. Misanthrope and misotheos by definition, isolated
from the outside world, he gradually consumes himself'. (Nos.29, 60, 174).
The total isolation of this broken and outcast figure brings the metaphor of
captivity, the title of this essay, out of the labyrinth of endless inquiries
into form and composition back to the central question: what is the
meaning and future of a human existence that is totally encapsulated in
itself because it is no longer capable of human contact and social fulfilment? It is these figures that establish Fuseli's significance as an artist at
the turn of the nineteenth century. But they also point forward to our day.

Fig.20 Edvard Munch, *Puberty*
(Oslo, Nationalgalerie)

To what extent Fuseli anticipated the trauma of bourgeois self-destruction can be seen from a comparison with Edvard Munch. A few examples
are enough to prove the point. A century after Fuseli, Munch rediscovered
frontality as a means of suggesting the fearful, questioning attitude of his
figures. There is, however, no evidence to suggest that he knew or used
Fuseli's prototypes[7]. If we compare Munch's 'Puberty' (fig.20), inspired by
Rops[8], with Fuseli's 'Fear' (No.174), the similarity in mood is apparent.
The figure's frontality destroys the internal unity of the composition. The
disjointedness which we considered to be the shortcoming of a number of
Fuseli's multi-figure compositions now becomes a legitimate, even essential symbol of the breakdown of communication. Withdrawal from the
world as a result of disappointment or bitterness links, for instance,
'Ugolino' (fig.10) and 'Lady Constance' (No.29) with Munch's 'Ashes'
(fig.21). Fuseli chooses the moment when Lady Constance sees her plans
to gain the throne for her son by artifice about to fail. He portrays her as
the avenging female she herself describes in her monologue:

Fig.21 Edvard Munch, *Ashes*,
lithograph

> To me and to the state of my great grief
>
> Let kings assemble; for my grief's so great
>
> That no supporter but the huge firm earth
>
> Can hold it up: here I and sorrows sit;
>
> Here is my throne, bid kings come bow to it.

(Shakespeare, King John, III, 1, 70–74)

Gustav Svenaeus has remarked of Munch's 'Ashes' that the woman's
features 'do not reflect the attitude of the femme fatale. What they express is not superiority and indifference, but isolation and despair. Not
only the man symbolises defeat. The woman, too, mourns the fading of
love'[9]. In Munch's 'Paraphrase of Salome' the arms and flowing hair of the
femme fatale encircle the head of a man whose features are not concealed
by any heroic mask': he is, quite simply, fin-de-siècle bourgeois man. The
woman's face is hidden from view, but the way she all but devours the
man contains echoes of Fuseli's 'Silence' (No.98). Munch develops one of
Fuseli's basic themes, the relationship between a man and a woman, and
sets it down as an ornamental symbol. The connexion between Fuseli's
'Nightmare' (No.159) and Munch's 'The Day After' (fig.22) may not be
immediately apparent. The link is provided by the lithograph 'Desire'

Cat.159 Fuseli, *The Nightmare*

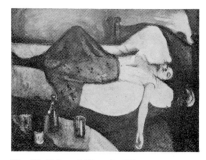

Fig.22 Edvard Munch, *The Day After*
(Oslo Nationalgalerie)

Fig.23 John Buscema and Joe Sinnott, *The Silver Surfer*

Fig.24 Fuseli, *The Executioner* (Weimar Staatliche Kunstsammlungen)

Fig.25 Jack Kirby, *Thor*

Cat.125 Fuseli, *Thor Battering the Midgard Serpent*

in which three grotesque, lecherous monsters are gazing at the delicate body of a girl not unlike that in Fuseli's painting. In 'The Day After' incubation has already taken place, the spectre has vanished, nevertheless Munch gives the theme a twist that distinguishes it from Fuseli's version; namely, he secularises it, intensifies it by removing it from the world of ghosts to the world of the psyche. What previously was carried out by monsters is now taken over by the instinct for self-destruction.

What has become of the other Fuseli, the choreographer of violence and catastrophe and the inventor of daring anatomical displays? The complex world of Fuseli's supermen lives on today in a sphere not generally taken seriously by art historians, namely in adventure strips[10]. This art historical prejudice effectively blocks the possibility of any research being conducted into the continued survival in vulgarised form of the humanistic cycles of gods and heroes. The draughtsmen engaged in this particular branch of anonymous consumer art adhere closely to the anatomical and illusionistic devices characteristic of Classicism and Mannerism that last appeared in Art in the work of Fuseli. Formal similarities are obvious; figures hovering or rotating in mid-air, the commanding pathos of the superman, the arrogant figure seen from behind – which Fuseli, as is well known, took from Andrea del Sarto's 'Beheading of John the Baptist' (figs. 23, 24), and the mythical symbol of universal destruction, Thor, who actively survives today (fig.25, No.125).

The problem of Fuseli's relevance to the present day therefore exists on two different levels. A close examination of his work reveals that both these levels have a direct bearing on the predicament of civilised man in today's civilization; on the one hand the hollow seclusion of introversion, on the other, the physical frenzy of extroversion. Both, whether they be captives of the ego or the compulsive need for action, are trying to escape.

[1] See Hofmann 'Zu Füsslis geschichtlicher Stellung' in *Zeitschrift für Kunstgeschichte*, 1952, p. 163ff.

[2] Heinrich Füssli, *Aphorismen über die Kunst*, publ. Walter Muschg, Basle, 1944.

[3] Otto Weigmann, *Moritz von Schwind*, Stuttgart-Leipzig, 1906 (Klassiker der Kunst), p. 376ff. – The Mannerists were already concerned with related anatomical explorations, albeit without expressly adhering to some unalterable pattern. See etchings of Juste de Juste in Henri Zerner, *Die Schule von Fontainebleau: Das graphische Werk*, Vienna – Munich, 1969, 1–5. Sylvie Beguin has pointed out the expression of pain in these 'pyramids' (*Revue de l'Art*, 5, 1969, p.103).

[4] See Schiff, p.192ff.

[5] David V. Erdman: *The Illuminated Blake*.

[6] Schiff has shown that Saul was modelled on an antique relief, the so-called 'Bacchante morante', in Florence. Goya was in Rome probably in 1770, and certainly by 1771. A visit to Florence is quite possible, as he returned to Spain via Northern Italy. Another possible source is an engraving by Reinier Vinkeles – 'Young Enterrant Sa Fille – in a popular French prose translation of *Night Thoughts* (1796). (Repr. in Marianne Löfström 'The Star and the Night' in *Contributions to the History and Theory of Art*, Uppsala, 1967, p. 127.) For the connection between Goya and the *Night Thoughts* see Peter Kühn-Nielsen in *Master Drawings*, 2, 1974, pp. 151 ff.

[7] On frontality: W. H., 'Zu einem Bildmittel Edvard Munchs' in *Alte und Neue Kunst*, 3, 1954, p.20ff. – In his book *Im männlichen Gehirn*, Lund 1973, Gösta Svenaeus often mentions relationships between Blake and Munch. It is therefore possible that Blake's frontality influenced Munch, see Plate 51 of 'Jerusalem' (Erdman op. cit. p.330) for the Salome paraphrase.

[8] Svenaeus: *Idé och Innehall in Edvard Munchs Konst*, Oslo, 1953, p.19.

[9] Svenaeus: *Im männlichen Gehirn*, p.228.

[10] Compare with W. H., 'Zu kunsthistorischen Problemen der Comic Strips in: *Vom Geist der Superhelden: Comic Strips. Zur Theorie der Bildergeschichte*, publ. Hans Dieter Zimmermann, Munich 1973, p.64ff. (From the proceedings of The Akademie der Künste, 8, Berlin, 1970, p.47ff.).

Biographical Outline

1741

6 February. Born in Zurich, second son of Johann Caspar Füssli the Elder (1706–1782), painter, town clerk and writer on art, and his wife Elisabeth, née Waser. The landscape painter Salomon Gessner is his godfather. All five children being artistically talented, Johann Caspar refers to his family as 'domus Fueslinorum, artis pingendi cultrix'.

Johann Caspar Fuseli, *Self-Portrait Aged 30*

1751ff.

First surviving drawings, copies of works by Tobias Stimmer, Jost Ammann, Gotthard Ringgli, German and Netherlandish masters, as well as some fantastic compositions of his own. Extensive art historical training under his father, who in 1755–7 publishes his *Geschichte und Abbildungen der besten Maler in der Schweiz*. He is also a staunch supporter of Mengs and Winckelmann and the spread of Neo-classical ideas in the German-speaking world. Fuseli's father allows him to assist in the preparation of his art history books, but decides he should become a Zwinglian minister. During his theoretical studies Johann Heinrich develops a certain hatred of dogma. Influence of Bodmer and his republican outlook, based on English liberalism.

Through Bodmer Fuseli becomes acquainted with Lavater, Felix Hess, Usteri, Pestalozzi. Bodmer also introduces him to the works of Homer, Dante, Shakespeare, Milton and the Nibelungenlied, which subsequently provide his main source of subject matter. Under the guidance of Breitinger, he becomes an accomplished classical philologist.

Fuseli, *Portrait of Johann Jakob Bodmer* (London, National Portrait Gallery)

1761

Ordination as Zwinglian minister. First sermon. Causes a stir by combining biblical criticism in the spirit of the Enlightenment with the new 'emotional' theology.

1762

Together with Lavater produces a pamphlet protesting against the extortionate administration of the Magistrate Grebel. They are summoned before the City Council and unofficially advised to leave Zurich for a while.

1763

With Lavater and Hess visited various towns in Germany. Extended stay in Berlin with the Swiss mathematician and art theorist Johann Georg Sulzer. Frederick the Great strikes him as the epitome of a tyrant and Germany, dismembered by petty principalities, as the prime example of an enslaved country. On 3 May Fuseli, Lavater and Hess travel to Barth in Pomerania where they spend several months with the Protestant theologian and moral philosopher Johann Joachim Spalding, possibly the happiest period in Fuseli's life. At the beginning of October he is summoned to Berlin by Sulzer who wants his assistance on his treatise on the fine arts, *Allgemeinen Theorie der schönen Künste*. His separation from Lavater affects Fuseli deeply. He gives expression to his emotions in a sentimental prose

Fuseli, *Lavater and Hess as Guests of Spalding at Barth*, engraving by Christian Ivon Mechel

poem, 'Klagen' (Complaints):

> Friend of my soul! The vanished hours of that early life we spent hand in
> hand passed then as in a vision before my eyes, ushered by the guardian
> spirit. Those blessed hours of our growing friendship, when I was every-
> thing to you; when, in my lap, you unfolded your first great thoughts and
> were called my dove! The mighty hours, wherein I learnt at your side that
> virtue is not just an idea, that the bliss of drying the tears of the unfor-
> tunate is more than a poet's dream, that fatherland and freedom are not
> evanescent echoes. . . . (Translated by Mason, 1951, p.99)

1764

Travels to London with Sir Andrew Mitchell, the English chargé d'affaires
in Berlin. His intellectual mentors, Bodmer, Breitinger and Sulzer, have
singled him out to act as mediator between English and German literatures.
He feels equally drawn to art and the theatre.

1765

Publishes an English translation of Winckelmann's *Reflections on the Paintings and Sculptures of the Greeks*. It finds little acclaim with the public and
is given curt, unfavourable reviews by the critics.

Title-page of Fuseli's translation of
Winckelmann's *Reflections on the
Painting and Sculpture of the Greeks*
(Zurich Bibliothek des Schweizerischen
Instituts fur Kunstwissenschaft)

1766

Travels to France as tutor to the 14 year-old Lord Chewton. Meets Jean-
Jacques Rousseau and David Hume in Paris. He writes to Bodmer in
Lyons on 7 February 1766: 'I spent a few hours with him (Rousseau) and
was as happy as a man can be'. He frees himself from the sentimental culti-
vation of virtue and the last vestiges of dogmatism. In Lyons he refuses to
baptise the child of a fellow Swiss.

1767

Publishes his *Remarks on the Writings and Conduct of J. J. Rousseau*, however it is scarcely noticed by the critics. Disappointed with Rousseau,
whom he feels has compromised himself by the quarrel with Hume, Fuseli
now rejects his ideas for social and political reform as utopian:

> There is a point from which no nation, if once arrived at, ever retro-
> grades. Where laws are only the curb of a public, the attempt of trans-
> fusing them into manners is folly; and where force is the only check upon
> the conflict of social interests, the most subtle impostor is the best politi-
> cian. Then you must change virtue to appearances, and give the pension
> of honesty to talent; then you must apply emollients, palliatives, call in
> arts, luxury, commerce, and the phantom of private and national honour.
> By their glittering advantages and insidious charms, you must bribe or
> sooth to slavery those you dread, dismember the rabble, and seizing every
> opportunity, throw out tubs to let their rage evaporate in harmless play.
> You must, *like Colbert*, feed the hungry with flowers, or with *Cato* repeat,
> 'Destroy Carthage!'

(Remarks on Rousseau, Mason 1962, p.138)

Fuseli adopts Rousseau's ideas about the arts endangering the state and
corrupting morals. These eventually lead him to uphold the total separation of art and morals. Clear indications of Fuseli's subsequent amoral attitude to his art which he intended to appeal only to a select circle of initiates.

1768

Meets Sir Joshua Reynolds who encourages him to become a painter.

1769

Work on a *History of German Poetry*, but the manuscript is destroyed in a
fire the following year.

Frontispiece of Fuseli's *Remarks on the
Writings and Conduct of J. J. Rousseau*,
engraving by Charles Grignion

1770

Goes to Italy to train as a painter. Reaches Genoa at the end of April. After
a stay in Florence, arrives in Rome at the end of May. He soon opposes
himself to the fashionable artistic circles in Rome:

> The man who was so praised by the truly great Winckelmann, namely the
> world famous Mengs, was not worthy of the name he gave him; he is not
> worthy now, and posterity, which can judge impartially, will be amazed
> that a man could have written so respectably on art who included a
> mediocre artist along with Phidias and Apelles; for posterity will not
> know that gratitude has struck him blind.

(Letter to Lavater, 30 July 1770)

After his initial rejection of Michelangelo under the influence of Winckelmann, Fuseli finds the decisive models for his figure drawing in classical art
and in the Sistine Chapel.

Fuseli, drawing after Michelangelo

1772

Suffers from some feverish illness which leaves him shaking slightly in both
hands. Goes to Venice for a rest cure. Makes the acquaintance of the sculptors Sergel and Banks, and the painters Alexander Runciman, Nicolai
Abraham Abildgaard, John Romney, James Northcote, and John Brown.
He influences them all by his choice of themes from classical and northern
mythology, Shakespeare and Milton, and by his expressive, daringly simplified style. He becomes virtually leader of a school of painting. Despite the
claim in earlier literature on Fuseli, there is no documentary evidence of
any contact between him and Jacques-Louis David, who arrived in Rome
in 1775.

Sergel, bust of Fuseli (Stockholm,
Nationalmuseum)

1773

On 31 July Thomas Banks reported to London: 'Among the students in
Painting, Fuseli cuts the greatest figure; last season he had pictures bespoke
to the amount of 1300 l., . . . nothing more than, from his great abilities, he
is justly entitled to.' Lavater provides the German Sturm und Drang
artists and writers with information about Fuseli in Rome. In a letter to
Herder on 4 November 1773 Lavater describes him as follows:

> He is everything in extremes – always an original; His look is lightning,
> his word a thunderstorm; his jest is death, his revenge, hell.
> He cannot draw a *single* mean breath. He never draws portraits, his fea-
> tures are all true, yet at the same time caricature. . .

Goethe writes to Herder on 25 March 1775: What fire and fury the man
has in him!

Sergel, caricature of Fuseli in Rome
(Stockholm, Nationalmuseum)

1775

Stays in Naples. Visits the excavations in Pompeii and Herculaneum.

1778

Leaves Rome, arriving in Zurich in October. Works there on a painting of
The Three Confederates (*The Rütlischwur*) in the town hall (Nos.16 and 17).
Resumes his friendship with Lavater. Flirts with Magdalena Schweizer-
Hess (Nos.4, 176), falls passionately in love with Anna Landolt (No.159
verso). Her father's rejection of his suit causes him to return to London.

1780ff.

Fuseli makes his name in artistic and intellectual circles in England. He
frequents the circle of radical intellectuals that gathered round the book-
seller Joseph Johnson. However he also pursues more conservative contacts
such as the banker Thomas Coutts, the Locks of Norbury, and the banker
William Roscoe of Liverpool, who was also a Renaissance historian, art

Fuseli, *Portrait of Magdalena
Schweizer-Hess* (Weimar, Staatliche
Kunstsammlungen)

Shee, *Portrait of William Roscoe*
(Liverpool, Walker Art Gallery)

Fuseli, frontispiece to *Aphorisms
on Man*

John Opie, *Portrait of Mary
Wollstonecraft*

Felix Maria Diogg, *Johann Caspar
Lavater* (Switzerland, Private
collection)

collector and spokesman in the fight against the slave trade. In 1781 Fuseli scores his first world-wide success with his painting of 'The Nightmare'. The publication between 1781 and 1786 of the French edition of Lavater's *Physiognomische Fragmente* containing Fuseli's illustrations, increases his fame. In 1786, together with Romney, the landscapist Paul Sandby, Benjamin West and others, he is invited to a dinner party by the Lord Mayor of London, the print publisher John Boydell, at which the idea of the 'Shakespeare Gallery' is conceived. All noteworthy artists in England are to be involved in the enterprise. The aim is to pave the way for historical painting in England by producing a cycle of paintings of scenes from Shakespeare to be circulated as engravings on the continent. Up to the opening of the first exhibition of the 'Shakespeare Gallery' in 1789, Fuseli devotes most of his time and energies to this work.

c.1787
Beginning of his friendship with William Blake. Their initial intense exchange of ideas is restricted by Fuseli's objections to Blake's mysticism.

1788
On 30 July marries Sophia Rawlins from Bath-Easton near Bath. (c.f. Nos.5, 165, 177–183). Publication of *Aphorisms on Man*, a free translation of one of Lavater's manuscripts. On 3 November Fuseli is elected an Associate Member of the Royal Academy. In return he donates his painting of 'Thor Battering the Midgard Serpent' (No.125). In Johnson's *Analytical Review* Fuseli writes anonymous reviews of exhibitions at the Royal Academy and the 'Shakespeare Gallery', which gives him ample opportunity to lavish praise on his own work. About his painting of 'Theseus Receiving the Thread from Ariadne' (No.55), he writes:

> Mythology can claim little of this performance besides the name. Its sentiment springs in every age, and dwells in every breast. That this Theseus was not fed with roses, that this Ariadne is worthy to be courted by a God, is their smallest praise. If this be a sketch, it will be difficult to find a finished picture in the room.

1789
He writes the following comments on his painting of 'Titania, Bottom and the Fairies' (No.26):

> This is the creation of a poetic painter . . . The soft and insinuating beauty, the playful graces here displayed would, without reflection, scarcely be expected from the daring pencil that appears ever on the stretch to reach the upmost boundary of nature.

(*Analytical Review*, IV, May 1789, p.110; Mason p.289).

Fuseli meets Mary Wollstonecraft, the revolutionary writer and advocate of women's rights. Three months after the storming of the Bastille Fuseli describes the period as '. . . an age pregnant with the most gigantic efforts of character, shaken with the convulsions of old, and the emergence of new empires: whilst an unexampled vigour seemed to vibrate from pole to pole through the human mind, and to challenge the general sympathy'. (*Analytical Review*, V, December 1789, pp.463–4, review of Coxe's *Travels in Switzerland*; Mason p.183f.)

1790
10 February. Fuseli is elected a full Member of the Royal Academy. Temporary disagreement with Reynolds who had favoured another candidate. In his review of Coxe's *Travels in Switzerland* Fuseli defends Lavater against Coxe's attacks on his leanings towards a belief in miracles and his

'magnetic' healing powers:

> If Mr. Lavater be weak enough to tamper with *animal magnetism*, he is certainly too wise to mix it with his religious tenets; but a belief in the 'efficacy of absolute faith' is if we are not mistaken, a belief in the text of that gospel, whose champion the *Rector of Bemerton* (Coxe) professes himself, and whose mysteries and miracles are surely not circumscribed by those narrow limits of self-conceited reason which he prescribes to a man whose faith is tempered by the most unremitting exertions of Christian duty, by melting charity and universal benevolence.

(*Analytical Review*, VI, February 1790, p.156ff.; Mason, p.140f.)

Fuseli decides to emulate the collective work of the 'Shakespeare Gallery' with a series of over thirty illustrations to Milton, the 'Milton Gallery', executed by him alone (c.f. Nos.86–91, 96–105). For this project he gains the moral and financial support of both William Roscoe and Johnson.

1791

In his review of Reynolds' last Discourse Fuseli makes the following remark on Reynolds' famous theory of imitation:

> It is a mind similar to Michelangelo alone, that can ever make use of him (i.e. his forms): but he who can imitate him will hardly condescend to copy.

(*Analytical Review*, X, May 1791, p.4; Mason, p.212.)

1792

Publication of a three volume English edition of Lavater's *Physiognomische Fragmente* by Fuseli's friend, Johnson. Fuseli was involved in the project, supervising the translation and the engravings, altering some of his own comments on the illustrations, and writing an introduction. In it he totally ignores Lavater's premise that physiognomy should have a religious basis. He describes the perception of character from facial characteristics as an intuitive ability possessed by all men. He emphasises that Lavater is concerned exclusively with physiognomy, not pathognomy, that he bases his deductions solely on the original forms of the skull and face and not on the distortion of features caused by the emotions. In this he was siding with Lavater against Lichtenberg who refused to acknowledge the validity of anything but pathognomy. Fuseli's attitude is in keeping with his theory of art, for he considers the highest aim of painting to be the depiction of human nature freed from all individual blemishes.

Fuseli, illustration for the English edition of Lavater's *Physiognomy*

Plans to go to Paris with Johnson and Mary Wollstonecraft, who has fallen passionately in love with him, to witness the Revolution with their own eyes. In the end Mary Wollstonecraft travels to Paris alone when Mrs Fuseli puts an end to her flirtation with her husband.

1793

Fuseli works tirelessly at his 'Milton Gallery'. Gets involved in a hefty controversy with the Rev. R. A. Bromley, a dilettantish writer on art and friend of Benjamin West. The previous year West had been appointed President of the Royal Academy. In his review of Bromley's *Philosophical and Critical History of the Fine Arts* Fuseli openly admits his amoral approach to aesthetics:

R. M. Wardle, *Portrait of Mary Wollstonecraft*, engraving after a painting by Opie

> It is ludicrous to give a consequence to the arts which they can never possess. Their moral usefulness is at best accidental and negative. It is their greatest praise to furnish the most innocent amusement for those nations to whom luxury is become as necessary as existence, and amongst whom alone they can rear themselves to any degree of eminence.

(*Analytical Review*, XVI, July 1793, pp.242–3; Mason p.193)

Lawrence, *Portrait of Fuseli aged 55*, engraving by Thomas Holloway

Blake, illustration for Edward Young's *Night Thoughts* (London, British Museum)

Lawrence, *Satan Calling his Legions* (Royal Academy of Arts)

After the execution of Louis XVI, the English declaration of war with France and the suppression of the Girondists by the Jacobins, Fuseli and various other moderate intellectuals become opponents of the Revolution:

He who reads the works of Tacitus according to the arrangement with which they have been transmitted to us by all the editors, will find that they inculcate the important and terrible maxim, that anarchy is the legitimate offspring of despotism, and that the tools of oppression end in becoming the engines of revolution. If the people be such as Tacitus describes, the dregs of a nation brought up by liberty, perverted by conquest, and overwhelmed by its own weight, sinking into despotism, the anarchies that ensue will be little more than the temporary contests for rule of factions equally criminal; and the vital sparks of public virtue being in such a nation entirely extinguished, and that of private energy reduced to a tame remembrance of antiquated heroism, the bulk will subside again under the tyrant of the ruling party, and in degenerate silence subscribe to the law of force.

(*Analytical Review*, XVII, November 1793, review of Murphy's *Tacitus*, p.242f.; Mason p.184f.)

1795

The historian William Seward, the art collector William Lock, and the Shakespeare critic George Steevens promise to support Fuseli's work on the 'Milton Gallery'.

1796

Fuseli reviews Roscoe's *Life of Lorenzo de' Medici* in the *Analytical Review*. Roscoe increases his support of the 'Milton Gallery'. Fuseli writes an anonymous introduction to an edition of Young's *Night Thoughts* with illustrations by William Blake.

1798

Roscoe introduces him to the engraver Moses Haughton.

1799

20 May: opening of the 'Milton Gallery' exhibition at Christies in Pall Mall. Well received by Fuseli's colleagues at the Royal Academy, especially by Thomas Lawrence, his staunchest admirer among English painters. However the public remains indifferent, and Fuseli is forced to close the exhibition prematurely at the end of July.

Fuseli applies for the post of Professor of Painting at the Royal Academy; he is elected on 29 June with a two-thirds majority. Visits Liverpool with Johnson and Roscoe.

1800

'Milton Gallery' reopened on 21 March with seven additional paintings. Public support again lacking. To boost the numbers of visitors various members of the Royal Academy organise a banquet in Fuseli's honour. After the closure of the exhibition friends such as the Countess of Guilford. Lord Rivers, Thomas Coutts, John Julius Angerstein, among others, buy some of the main works.

In his diary entry for 2 May Goethe writes: 'One may say of Fuseli, as of every mannerist of genius, that he parodies himself'. Goethe accuses Fuseli of 'addressing himself to the imagination' which should be the sole prerogative of the poet, – 'thereby using sensuous representation only as a vehicle . . . With Fuseli, poetry and painting are always at war with one another . . . one values him as a poet, but as a plastic artist he always makes his audience impatient. . . Manner in everything, especially in anatomy, therefore also in the attitudes.'

1801

Fuseli begins work as Professor of Painting at the Royal Academy by holding a series of three lectures on 'Ancient Art', 'Art of The Moderns' and 'Invention'. The following excerpts demonstrate his predominantly classicist outlook as a theoretician:

> ... by *nature* I understand the general and permanent principles of visible objects, not disfigured by accident, or distempered by disease, not modified by fashion or local habits. Nature is a collective idea, and, though its essence exist in each individual of the species, can never in its perfection inhabit a single object.

(Lecture I in John Knowles, *The Life and Writings of Henry Fuseli* II, London 1831, p.21; Mason, p.231f.)

> Of *genius* I shall speak with reserve, for no word has been more indiscriminately confounded; by genius I mean that power which enlarges the circle of human knowledge, which discovers new materials of nature or combines the known with novelty, whilst *talent* arranges, cultivates, polishes the discoveries of genius.

(Lecture I, Knowles II, p.23; Mason p.317)

> ... the term *invention* never ought to be so far misconstrued as to be confounded with that of *creation*, incompatible with our notions of limited being, an idea of pure astonishment, and admissible only when we mention Omnipotence: to *invent* is to find: to find something presupposes its existence somewhere, implicitly or explicitly, scattered or in a mass ...
>
> Form in its widest meaning, the visible universe that envelops our senses, and its counterpart, the invisible one that agitates our mind with visions bred on sense by fancy, are the element and the realm of invention; it discovers, selects, combines the *possible*, the *probable*, the *known*, in a mode that strikes with an air of truth and novelty, at once.

(Lecture III, Knowles II, p.136ff.; Mason, p.201f.)

> ... the Greeks carried the art to a height which no subsequent time or race has been able to rival or even to approach.

(Lecture I, Knowles II, p.25; Mason, p.224)

In his second Lecture on 'Art of the Moderns' Fuseli describes Michelangelo as the painter of human nature in general, and Raphael as the painter of individual humanity and the father of dramatic painting:

> (Michelangelo) is the inventor of epic painting, in that sublime circle of the Sistine Chapel which exhibits the origin, the progress, and the final dispensations of theocracy. He has personified motion in the groups of the cartoon of Pisa ("The Battle of Cascina"); embodied sentiment on the monuments of St. Lorenzo, unravelled the features of meditation in the Prophets and Sybils of the Sistine Chapel; and in the *Last Judgement*, with every attitude that varies the human body, traced the master-trait of every passion that sways the human heart.

(Lecture II, Knowles, p.85; Mason, p.249)

Lavater dies on 2 February. Fuseli plans to write a biography of his friend, but gives it up, probably because of the deep-rooted religious and philosophical conflict that had developed between them in later years.

1802

Fuseli writes – in this order – Lecture VII ('On Design'), Lectures VIII and IX ('Colour: In Fresco Painting' and 'Colour: Oil Painting'), and Lecture V ('Composition, Expression').

Lecture VII contains the following contribution to the theory of eclecticism:

> It must however be owned, that he would commit a more venial error, and come nearer to the form we require in the Achilles of Homer, who

Title-page of the first edition of Fuseli's *Lectures on Painting* (Zurich, Zentralbibliothek)

Fuseli, *Pedagog and the Youngest Son of Niobe* (Zurich, Kunsthaus)

David, *Belisarius* (Paris, Musée du Louvre)

[44]

Sebastiano del Piombo, *The Martyrdom of St. Agatha* (Florence, Palazzo Pitti)

A. van Ostade, *The Pig Slaughter*, an example of the loathsome depiction of horror defined by Fuseli in Lecture V

Murillo, *The Lousecatcher* (Paris, Louvre)

Antoine Denis Chaudet, *Belisarius* (Chateau de Malmaison)

should substitute the form of the Apollo or Hercules with the motion of the Gladiator to the real form, than he who should copy him from the best individual he could meet with: the reason is clear; there is a greater analogy between their form and action and that of Achilles, than between him and the best model we know alive.

(Lecture VII, Knowles II, p.324; Mason, p.233)

In Lecture VIII he declares drawing to be superior to colour when discussing the object of the Arts, and how it is essential that they: make sense the minister of mind . . . *Design*, in its most extensive as in its strictest sense, is their basis; when they stoop to be the mere playthings, or debase themselves to be the debauchers of the senses, they make *Colour* their insidious foundation . . . It is not for me, (who have courted and still continue to court Colour as a despairing lover courts a disdainful mistress,) to presume, by adding my opinion, to degrade the great one [Reynolds] delivered; but the attachments of fancy ought not to regulate the motives of a teacher, or direct his plan of art: it becomes me therefore to tell you, that if the principle which animates the art gives rights and privilege to Colour not its own; . . . if what is claimed in vain by form and mind, it fondly grants to colour; . . . then the art is degraded to a mere vehicle of sensual pleasure, an implement of luxury, a beautiful *but trifling* bauble, or a splendid fault.

(Knowles II, pp.332–4; Mason, p.261)

In Lecture V he explains his interpretation of the allegorical nature of mythology:

Only then, when passion and suffering become too big for utterance, the wisdom of ancient art has borrowed a feature from tranquillity, though not its air. For every being seized by an enormous passion, be it joy or grief, or fear sunk to despair, loses the character of its own individual expression, and is absorbed by the power of the feature that attracts it. Niobe and her family are assimilated by extreme anguish; Ugolino is petrified by the fate that swept the stripling at his foot, and sweeps in pangs the rest. The metamorphoses of ancient mythology are founded on this principle, are allegoric. Clytia, Biblis, Salmacis, Narcissus, tell only the resistless power of sympathetic attraction.

(Knowles II, p.259f.; Mason, p.305)

Fuseli goes on to define the difference between the legitimate depiction of terror and the inadmissible depiction of horror:

We cannot sympathise with what we detest or despise, nor fully pity what we shudder at or loathe . . . mangling is contagious, and spreads aversion from the slaughterman to the victim.

(Lecture V, Knowles II, p.262f.; Mason, p.217)

On 27 August Fuseli travels to Paris with the landscape painter Joseph Farington and others to study the works of art brought together in the Musée Napoléon. The English artists all unanimously reject David, both as an artist and as a human being; they even go as far as to view the works in his studio during his absence. They think highly of Gérard, Girodet, Guérin and the sculptor Chaudet. Fuseli meets Ennio Quirino Visconti, Charles Percier, Alexandre-Marie Lenoir; visits the opera; enjoys a reunion with his old friends Johann Caspar and Magdalena Schweizer-Hess; and studies the masterpieces in the Louvre in greatest detail. They return to London at the beginning of October.

1803

Fuseli considers Buonaparte a man buoyed up with pride and presumption and of unrestrained passion; and that he must suffer much in the

opinion of the world, by his conduct and deportment – He thinks the
War will be short.   (*Farington Diary*, 28 May 1803; Mason, p.186)

Moses Haughton comes to live with the Fuselis. He is to spend the next
fifteen years there. From this time on he is solely responsible for the engravings made after Fuseli's paintings.

1804

Lecture IV ('Invention, Part II').

Benjamin Robert Haydon becomes Fuseli's pupil. In his autobiography
Haydon looks back on his initial impression of Fuseli:

> I found him the most grotesque mixture of literature, art, scepticism,
> indelicacy, profanity and kindness. He reminded me of Archimago (the
> evil magician in Spenser's *Faerie Queene*). Weak minds he destroyed.
> They mistook his wit for reason, his indelicacy for breeding, his swearing
> for manlinness, and his infidelity for strength of mind; but he was
> accomplished in elegant literature, and had the art of inspiring young
> minds with high and grand views. . .

(Tom Taylor, ed., *Life and Autobiography of Benjamin Robert Haydon,
Historical Painter, from his Autobiography and Journals*, 2nd ed., 3 vols.,
London 1853, I, p.33; Mason, p.74f.)

1804

24 December, Fuseli is elected Keeper to the Royal Academy.

1805

He resigns as Professor of Painting. His greatly revised edition of Matthew
Pilkington's dictionary of artists is published, an important step in the
direction of a less doctrinaire and more historical approach to art history.
He meets his future biographer and friend, John Knowles.

In his signed preface to *Blair's Grave*, illustrated by Blake, Fuseli writes
among other things, that not only Blake's invention but also his technique
and execution 'claim approbation'.

> [It] sometimes excite[s] our wonder, and not seldom our fears, when we
> see him play on the very verge of legitimate invention. But wildness so
> picturesque in itself, so often redeemed by taste, simplicity and elegance,
> what child of fancy, what artist would wish to discharge? The groups and
> single figures, on their own bases, abstracted from the general composi-
> tion and considered without attention to the plan, frequently exhibit
> those genuine, unaffected attitudes, those simple graces, which Nature
> and the heart alone can dictate, and only an eye inspired by both dis-
> cover. Every class of artist, in every stage of their progress or attain-
> ments, from the student to the finished master, and from the contriver of
> ornament to the painter of history, will find here material of art and hints
> of improvement!

(Knowles I, p.293ff.; Mason, p.287f.)

1806

An anonymous critic in *Bell's Weekly Messenger* attacks Fuseli's painting
of 'Ugolino' then on exhibition at the Academy (No.121). On 1 July
William Blake writes the following reply in a letter published in *The
Monthly Magazine*:

> . . . such an artist as Fuseli is invulnerable, he needs not my defence;
> but I should be ashamed not to set my hand and shoulder, and whole
> strength, against those wretches who, under pretence of criticism, use
> the dagger and the poison. . . My criticism of the picture is as follows:
> Mr Fuseli's Count Ugolino is the father of sons of feeling and dignity,
> who would not sit looking in their parent's face in the moment of his
> agony, but would rather retire and die in secret, while they suffer him to

Haydon, *Self-Portrait* (National
Portrait Gallery)

Title-page of *Blair's Grave* illustrated
by William Blake (Munich, Private
collection)

*Ugolino and his Sons Starving to Death
in the Tower*, line engraving by
Moses Haughton after Fuseli
(Zurich, Kunsthaus)

indulge his passionate and innocent grief, his innocent and vulnerable madness and insanity and fury, and whatever paltry, cold-hearted critics cannot, because they dare not, look upon . . .

A gentleman who visited me the other day, said, 'I am very much surprised at the dislike that some connoisseurs shew on viewing the pictures of Mr. Fuseli; but the truth is, he is a hundred years beyond the present generation'. Though I am startled at such an assertion, I hope the contemporary taste will shorten the hundred years into as many hours . . .
(*The Poetry and Prose of William Blake*, ed. Geoffrey Keynes, London 1943, p.911)

1807

In recognition of his excellent teaching, Haydon presents Fuseli with a silver vase designed by Flaxman on behalf of the students at the Royal Academy.

Publication in Zurich of *Heinrich Füsslis Sämtliche Werke nebst einem Versuch seiner Biographie*, a monograph with sixteen outline engravings by Franz Hegi and Heinrich Lips and a text by Fuseli's childhood friend, the Chorherr H. Nüschler. It was not continued.

1808

Work on the 'History of Art in the Schools of Italy', which remained a fragment (published posthumously by Knowles in Vol.III of *The Life and Writings of Henry Fuesli*).

Linnell, *Portrait of William Blake*, watercolour (National Portrait Gallery)

1808–12

After some years of estrangement which had eventually led to the complete cessation of contact between the two men, Blake then writes the following famous verse about Fuseli in his notebook:

The only Man that e'er I knew

Who did not make me almost spew

Was Fuseli: he was both Turk & Jew –

And so, dear Christian Friends, how do you do?
('Rossetti Notebook'; Epigram No.69, in *Poetry and Prose of W. Blake*, ed. Keynes, p.551)

1809

Goethe revises his opinion of Fuseli's art in a letter to Heinrich Meyer on 9 September. He admits that he can learn 'a good deal that is historically interesting' from the new engravings after Fuseli's paintings.

Haydon, copy of Dionysos from the Parthenon

1810

Fuseli is re-elected Professor of Painting. To enable him to retain his other post of Keeper, the statutes of the Royal Academy are altered.

1812

Holds Lecture VI ('Chiaroscuro') for the first time.

1813

Following a 'nervous fever' with depressive side-effects he goes to Hastings with John Knowles to recuperate (c.f. Nos.162, 173).

1814

Haydon leaves Fuseli. His former disciple now finds him too blasphemous; and he cannot forgive his lack of support in the struggle for the recognition of the Parthenon Marbles which Lord Elgin brought to London shortly before. For a long time Fuseli could not decide whether to attribute these sculptures to Phidias or not; they seemed to him too realistic, and not timeless and ideal enough. The conflict is only resolved in Lecture X of 1822.

Fuseli, page from the manuscript of *Aphorisms 65* (Zurich Kunsthaus)

1816

At Canova's instigation, Fuseli is elected a member of the first class of the Academy of St. Luke in Rome.

1818

Fuseli completes the editing of his 'Aphorisms, Chiefly relative to the Fine Arts' on which he has worked intermittently since 1788. (published in Knowles, Vol.III).

An example:

> Consider it as the unalterable law of Nature that all your power upon others depends on your own emotions. Shakspeare wept, trembled, laughed first at what now sways the public feature; and where he did not, he is stale, outrageous or disgusting.

(Aphorism 200; Mason, p.344)

1820

Fuseli arranges the republication of his first three Lectures with the addition of Lectures IV, V and VI (as in Knowles II). He also provides a preface containing a critical survey of all important historiographers and art theorists. In it he pronounces the following judgement:

> Winckelmann was the parasite of the fragments that fell from the conversation or the tablets of Mengs . . . he reasoned himself into frigid reveries and Platonic dreams on beauty . . . To him Germany owes the shackles of her artists, and the narrow limits of their aim; from him they have learnt to substitute the means for the end, and by a hopeless chace after what they call beauty, to lose what alone can make beauty interesting, expression and mind.

(*A Characteristic Sketch of the Principal Instruction, Ancient and Modern, which we possess*, Knowles II, p.13f.; Mason, p.301)

1821–3

Edits his last three Lectures (X, 'The Method of fixing a Standard and defining the Proportions of the Human Frame, with Directions to the Student in Copying the Life'; XI, 'On the prevailing Method of treating the History of Painting, with Observations on the Picture of Lionardo da Vinci of "The Last Supper"': XII, 'On the Present State of the Art, and the Causes which check its Progress'), though they are based on drafts made earlier. They are characterised by a deep cultural pessimism. In Lecture X, Fuseli returns to an idea that he first mooted in his 'Remarks on Rousseau' back in 1767:

Moses Haughton, portrait miniature of Fuseli, 1822 (Switzerland, Private collection)

> Neither Poety nor Painting spring from the necessities of society, or furnish necessaries to life; offsprings of fancy, leisure and lofty contemplation, organs of religion and government, ornaments of society, and too often mere charms of the senses and instruments of luxury, they derive their excellence from novelty, degree and polish. What none indispensably want, all may wish for, but few only are able to procure, acquires its value from some exclusive quality, founded on intrinsic, or some conventional merit, and that, or an equal substitute, mediocrity cannot reach: . . . A good mechanic, a trusty labourer, an honest tradesman, are beings more important, of greater use to society, and better supporters of the state, than an artist or a poet of mediocrity. When I therefore say that it is the duty of the Academy to deter rather than to delude, I am not afraid of having advanced a paradox hostile to the progress of real Art. The capacities that time will disclose, genius and talents, cannot be deterred by the exposition of difficulties, and it is in the interest of society that all else should.

(Lecture X, Knowles II, p.390f.; Mason, p.197).

In a surprising re-emergence of the Christian and theological bias of his early years, Fuseli now sees the only hope of art becoming 'healthy' again, in its renewed association with religion:

> If the revolution of a neighbouring nation emancipated the people from the yoke of superstition, it has perhaps precipitated them to irreligion. He who has no visible object of worship is indifferent about modes, and rites, and places; and unless some great civil provisional establishment replaces the means furnished by the former system, the Arts of France, should they disdain to become the minions and handmaids of fashion, may soon find that the only public occupation left for them will be a representation of themselves, deploring their new- acquired advantages.

(Knowles III, p.51; Mason, p.167).

Artist unknown, *Fuseli's Studio in Somerset House* (Mrs M. C. Heath)

1825

At the beginning of April, Fuseli almost completes his painting of 'Lady Constance, Arthur and Salisbury' (Shakespeare, *King John*, III, 1; No.30). On 16 April he dies at the Countess of Guilford's country home at Putney Hill, in the presence of his wife, the Countess and her daughter, Knowles and possibly Sir Thomas Lawrence. On 25 April he is buried in St. Paul's between Sir Joshua Reynolds and John Opie, an honour normally only accorded by the Royal Academy to its Presidents.

Catalogue

The catalogue is divided into sections according to subject matter. (See Contents p.5.) Within each section oil paintings are listed first followed by drawings and prints.

The dating of the works is done in three ways. Where dated by Fuseli himself the date is shown without brackets; where the date is supported by documentary evidence it is placed in round brackets; where the date is arrived at on the basis of stylistic analysis, it is given in square brackets.

Greek inscriptions are rendered in Fuseli's spelling and punctuation.

Dimensions are given in centimetres, height preceding width.

The reference to a Schiff number for each entry accords to the catalogue number in Gert Schiff's Catalogue Raisonné *Johann Heinrich Füssli* (Zurich 1973).

1

Self-Portraits and Satires

JOHN OPIE

1   Portrait of Henry Fuseli 1794

Oil on canvas, 75 × 61.6 cm
London, Trustees of the National Portrait Gallery, Inv. No.744

This portrait by John Opie (1761–1807) remained after Fuseli's death in the possession of his wife. Unfortunately the companion portrait of Mrs Fuseli has since vanished. Both paintings were exhibited in the Royal Academy in 1794 as 'A Gentleman' and 'A Lady'. In 1801 Fuseli's portrait was engraved by Ridley for the *Monthly Mirror* and again in 1834 by G. Harlow. After Mrs Fuseli's death it came into the possession of the Countess of Guilford. In 1885 it was presented to the National Portrait Gallery by her heirs Lord North and Colonel North M.P.

2   Self-Portrait of the Artist [*c.*1777]

Black chalk, 32.4 × 50.2 cm
Inscr. on the right-hand side of the book in pencil: 'John Cartwright'; and on the box 'Mr I.C. box'
Schiff: 1743
London, Trustees of the National Portrait Gallery, Inv. No.4538

2

3

Opposite: *Half-length Figure of a Courtesan* (detail of catalogue No.190)

4

5

The sitter was identified by Nicolas Powell. This is substantiated by comparison with other self-portraits, especially Nos.3 and 9 as well as with later portraits of Fuseli by Singleton, Lawrence and Baily among others. The inscription 'John Cartwright' is not in Fuseli's handwriting and the initials on the box presumably refer to the landscape painter of that name. As the two men worked in close co-operation in Rome this is highly probable.

3   Self-Portrait Aged Between Forty and Fifty Years Old [1780–90]

Black chalk heightened with white,
27 × 20 cm
Inscr. bottom right by an unknown hand: 'Wickstead'
Lit: Powell 1951, 43; Praz 1952, p.33, with ill.; Antal 1952, p.260; Antal 1956, p.126, note 3; Tomory 1972, frontispiece
Schiff: 864; cf.No.2
London, Victoria and Albert Museum, Inv. No.E.1028-1918 (presented by Captain H. Reitlinger)

4   Fuseli Reading to the Hess Sisters 1778

Pen and ink, 36 × 30.9 cm
Inscr. bottom right: '22. Nov. 78'; collection stamp of the Countess of Guilford
Exh: Zurich 1926 (133), 1941 (264); London 1950 (47); Bremen/Dusseldorf 1957 (73); Zurich 1969 (160)
Lit: Federmann 1927, repr. p.131; Ganz 1947, No.31; Woodward 1950, p.360; Antal 1956, p.43; Schiff 1964 (2), p.159, repr.19
Schiff: 580
Zurich, Kunsthaus, Inv. No.1940/126 (formerly Paul Hürlimann)

During his six-month stay in Zurich on his way back from Rome Fuseli was a close friend of Magdalena and Martha Hess. Magdalena was married to the wealthy Johann Caspar Schweizer who, in his various guises as philanthropist, project planner, philosophical dreamer and spendthrift played a curious role in Parisian society before and after the Revolution. Magdalena was no less eccentric herself. She was a coquette, and of an irritable nervous constitution. She claimed she could divine earthquakes and underground springs, she could let herself go into an hypnotic trance by having her hair combed, she prophesied when in a feverish state etc. Martha was far more ethereal and tended towards religious ecstasy. She died of consumption shortly after Fuseli's departure in December 1779.

5   Portrait of Mrs Fuseli in a Red Cap 1794

Pencil with watercolour, 34.6 × 21.6 cm
Inscr. on her shawl: 'Aug. 94'
Lit: Schiff 1959, 30; Tomory 1972, repr. 203
Schiff: 1099
Belfast, Ulster Museum, Inv. No.3539 (VII)

6

6 Death of a Swedish Hussar 1764

Pen and wash, 22.5 × 37.4 cm
Inscr. at top with a foot (play on Fuseli's
name; German for foot = Fuss) and: 'Jan. 64';
inscribed on the paper hung on the wall at
top left: 'On the strict orders of his Imperial
Majesty of Sweden etc., etc., and the Pom-
eranian government, the light infantry and
hussars etc., etc., are strictly forbidden to
disembowel or rape. Any such inhuman
behaviour will be punished' (the rest is
illegible)
Exh: Zurich 1926 (87); 1941 (213); 1969 (125)
Lit: Ganz 1947, p.3; Antal 1956, pl.3b, p.13,
19, 29, 162
Schiff 1960, p.26
Schiff: 356
Zurich, Kunsthaus, Inv. No.1920/27

During a stay in the Swedish part of Pomerania
(from April or the beginning of May until September
1763) Fuseli struck up a lively friendship with the
theologian Johann Gottlieb Picht, who at the time
was military chaplain to Baron von Wrangel's yel-
low hussars stationed at Barth. The clergyman who
is assisting the dying hussar in this drawing seems
to be Picht (probably drawn from memory), as can
be proved by comparing the figure with Fuseli's
portrait sketch of Picht (Schiff 355). Fuseli trans-
forms what may have been a real and witnessed
incident into a grotesque and fantastic scene.

7

7 The Mad House [1772]

Pen and sepia with grey wash, 38 × 64 cm
Inscr. bottom right in pen: 'Fuseli. fec.'
Lit: Collins Baker/James 1933, repr. 112;
Powell 1951, No.35, p.41; Antal 1954, p.260f.;
Antal 1956, p.39
Schiff: 515
London, Trustees of the British Museum,
Inv. No.1907-11-6-4

The drawing is based on an incident Fuseli experienced in Rome. In the Hospital of S. Spirito he once
saw a dying man refuse communion and try to
escape from the monks who were the harbingers of
death. He used the composition again in his illustrations to Lavater's *Essays in Physiognomy* as well
as in 'The Vision of the Lazar House' (No.102).

**8 Two Men (Fuseli and an Unknown Artist)
'Smoking a Picture'** [1774]

Watercolour and sepia over pencil,
30.5 × 21.5 cm
Lit: Antal 1956, p.64, note 105; Ditchburn-
Bosch 1960, p.17 and repr.
Schiff: 567
London, Trustees of the British Museum
Roman Album, fol.63v, No.82, Inv. No.1885-
3-14-274

8

Two men, one corpulent, the other slim, stand before a painting on an easel. The former stains the surface of the picture with the smoke from his long pipe, while the latter squeezes the contents out of two tubes inscribed with the words 'beauty' and 'sublime'.

Leaning against the easel is a board covered with anatomical details: the deltoid muscle of the back, the extensor and flexor muscles of the arm and schema for stylised patterns of male abdominal muscles (inscribed: deltoid, extens., flex., linea alla [sic] term. umb. [termine umbilicale]'). Fuseli is clearly alluding to Hogarth's etching 'Time Smoking a Picture' of 1761, a subscription card for engravings after Hogarth's painting 'Sigismunda', in which Hogarth parodies the preference for old pictures merely because of their age. His 'Sigismunda' had been painted in response to the taste that paid extravagant sums for paintings like 'Corregio's' (actually Furini's) 'Sigismunda' and the subscription ticket carried on the war against connoisseurs and 'dark masters'.

In his caricature Fuseli outlines the ingredients necessary to make a painting popular with the public, the dark tonality of an old master; skilled draughtsmanship (in particular in anatomy) and themes which accorded to Burke's concept of beauty and sublime.

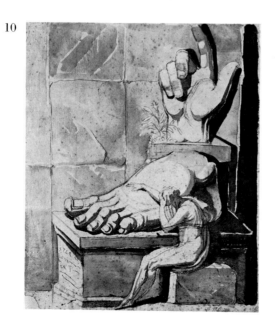

9

10

9   Second Allegory of Painting 1777

Pen over pencil, 30.5 × 22 cm
Inscr. bottom left: 'da Fuzely 1777'
On the back a sketch of a girl with a dagger
Exh: Zurich 1926 (113)
Lit: Schiff 1964, p.131f., repr. 87
Schiff: 493
Bischofszell in the Canton of Thurgau, Ernst Knoepfli-Biefer (formerly Frau Bassart-Looser, Zurich)

Like the 'Allegory of the Artist's Initiation into Painting' (Schiff 492) executed six years earlier, this second allegory throws light on a stage in Fuseli's progress towards artistic self-discovery. He draws himself as a painter identified by the mask, and as a 'man of the world' by the globe. The 'Vanitas' symbol of a rose blown from a bush emphasises the superficial, deceptive character of the world. The motif of the woman about to drive a nail into his head derives from the Biblical story of Jael and Sisera; this was generally used as an allegory of spiritual purification: taking Jael to represent the church and spirituality and Sisera carnal man. (*Silva, seu potius hortus floridus allegoriarum . .*) Autore P. Hieronimo Laureto . . . Cologne 1612.. The bandage over her mouth characterises the purifying force as 'Pictura', in other words, painting as mute poetry. Painting seizes Fuseli in her grip and teaches him how to overcome the world. What does this mean? Is it intended as a call to virtue as in

Michelangelo's 'Sogno', from which some of the motifs in Fuseli's drawing appear to derive? Does it thus symbolise the conquest of vanity and the desires of the flesh by spirituality and aesceticism? This hardly corresponds with Fuseli's thought and way of life in Rome. It presumably refers to a purely artistic decision: namely the artist's turning away from the world of appearances in order to devote himself to creating from his own imagination. The splitting open of his skull strikes one as a cruel but fitting image for the freeing of his imagination. Fuseli uses the complicated mechanism of the allegory, by then a dying genre, to convey what Blake expressed in a maxim in his *Laocoon Aphorisms* of 1815: 'Israel delivered from Egypt is Art delivered from Nature and Imitation'. At the same time, Fuseli also included his characteristic motif of male subjection to a cruel female task-mistress.

11

10 The Artist in Despair over the Magnitude of Antique Fragments (right hand and left foot of the Colossus of Constantine) [1778–80]

Red chalk and sepia wash, 42 × 35.2 cm
Inscr. bottom right false signature:
'85 W. Blake'; on the back, collection stamp
of the Countess of Guilford. Watermark 'ZP'
and the Zurich coat of arms
Exh: Zurich 1941 (251); New York 1954 (31);
Rome 1959 (226); Zurich 1969 (165)
Lit: Irwin 1966, p.47, repr. 32; Tomory
1972, repr. 4
Schiff: 665
Zurich Kunsthaus, Inv. No.1940/144
(formerly Paul Hürlimann)

12

11 Caricature of the Artist Leaving Italy (1778)

Pen and ink, 24.5 × 19.3 cm
Exh: Zurich 1969 (157)
Lit: Tomory 1972, repr. 1, p.50
Schiff: 568
Zurich, Kunsthaus, Inv. No.1938/668

The drawing depicts a nude antique hero half-squatting over a symbolic map of Europe, his stool dropping on Switzerland. In England he sees two skinny mice, the portraitists 'Humphry' and 'Romney', and a fat mouse, the court painter 'B. West'. His longing flies in the form of a phallic bird towards Italy.

Fuseli apparently enclosed this drawing in the letter he wrote in Lugano on 29 September 1778 to James Northcote who was staying on in Rome. Knowles (1831, I, pp.51–3) cites the letter from which this quotation comes: 'The enclosed I shall redemand at your hands in England. *Take heed of the mice!*' accompanied by the comment that it was satirical drawing of the painters in England at that time.

13

14

15

16

12 Deathbed or Sickbed of an Ancient Prince
(1752)

Pen and ink and wash over pencil,
14.9 × 27.8 cm
Inscr. at bottom: 'HF invenit 1752'
Schiff: 108
Zurich, Kunsthaus, Jugendalbum, pl.39 top

Possibly depicts the death of Antiochus Epiphanes
(2 Maccabees 9). An alternative suggestion is that it
represents Poseidonius who, visited by Pompeius
when suffering from gout, cried out that the pain
was raging in vain, for he would never admit that
pain was an evil. (Cicero, *Tusculanae disputationes*
II. 25; Strabo XI; Plutarch XXXII, 42.)

13 The Henpecked Husband [1757–9]

Pen and sepia with grey and pink wash,
16.3 × 12.1 cm
Inscr. bottom right: 'RM'; and beneath it the
lines: 'Du Narr dich reitet deine Stut|wardst
besattlet mit dem Weibergut' (You fool,
your mare rides you, you are saddled with
the dowry)
Beside this in red chalk '46'; the lining
inscribed at top '68'.
Lit: Antal, p.10
Schiff: 239
Zurich, Kunsthaus, Jugendalbum, sheet 62 top

This belongs to a group of twenty-nine drawings
Fuseli did between the age of sixteen and eighteen
which he claimed were copies after a fictive 'Narren-
buch' (Book of Fools) by the seventeenth century
Swiss artists Rudolf and Conrad Meyer and Gottfried Stadler.

14 Fool in a Fool's Cap (Eulenspiegel?) having
his Portrait Painted by a Bespectacled Artist
[1757–9]

Pen and sepia with grey greenish-ochre and
red-violet wash, 30.0 × 20.9 cm
Inscr. on the easel: 'J.H.F.'; beneath the
artist: 'R. Koch' (?); bottom right in red
chalk '55'
Lit: Schiff 1964 (2), p.151, repr. 12
Schiff: 259
Zurich, Kunsthaus, Jugendalbum, sheet 74

15 William Tell's Leap from the Ship [1758–60]

Pen and wash over pencil, 25.7 × 19.5 cm
Schiff: 266
Zurich, Kunsthaus, Inv. No.1940/85
(formerly Paul Hürlimann)

This is an episode from Schiller's legend of William
Tell. Tell had been seized by Gessler, the tyrannical
Austrian Governor of Altdorf and taken to his ship.
But when the ship ran into a storm on the lake of
Uri, the Austrian crew panicked. Tell, reputed to
be an able sailor, was taken to the helm. He rescued

the vessel and steered for the opposite coast, hoping
to escape. He brought the ship alongside a rock and
leapt for freedom.

16   The Confederates Arriving at the Rütli 1778

Pen and sepia wash with white highlights,
27.4 × 38.7 cm
Inscr. bottom right: 'Roma May 78'
Exh: London, Colnaghi's, *Old Master
Drawings*, 13–30 June 1967
Schiff: 1739
Zurich, Dr W. Amstutz (formerly Paul Grinke,
London)

This illustrates a famous episode in medieval Swiss
history when representatives of the three original
cantons swore in 1307 to free themselves from the
foreign yoke of Austria.

17   The Oath on the Rütli 1779

Pen and sepia, heightened with brown and
grey, 41.4 × 34.5 cm
Inscr. on a label: 'Zurico 79'; on the right: '3'
Exh: Zurich 1926 (135); 1941 (155); London
1950 (51); New York 1954 (4); Bremen/
Dusseldorf 1957 (70); Zurich 1969 (135)
Lit: Federmann 1927, p.50; Ganz 1947, p.29;
Antal 1956, p.71 ff., 91, pl.28; Irwin 1966,
pp.99–100, repr. 118
Schiff: 412
Zurich, Kunsthaus, Inv. No.1938/765

Preparatory study for Fuseli's painting in the Zurich Rathaus executed in 1780 (Schiff 359). For subject see No.16.

17

Shakespeare

18

20

21

18 Lady Macbeth Sleepwalking [1781–4]
(Shakespeare, *Macbeth*, V, 1)

Oil on canvas, 221 × 160 cm
Lit: Fuseli 1806, p.398; Horner 1826, p.10;
Anon. 1826, p.109; Fuseli 1842, p.164; Haydon
1853, I, p.25; Focillon 1927, p.24; Woodward
1950, p.111 ff., repr. 23; Antal 1956, p.93;
Merchant 1959, p.80; Monk 1960, p.201
Schiff: 738; cf. No.35
Paris, Musée du Louvre (formerly Carl Laszlo,
Basle; Richard Dreyfus, Basle; Paul Ganz,
Oberhofen)

Lady Macbeth, her conscience troubled by the evil
deeds done by herself and Macbeth, walks in her
sleep recounting these horrors watched by a waiting
gentlewoman and doctor of physic:
  Doct: How came she by that light?
  Gen: Why, it stood by her: she has light by her
  continually; 'tis her command.
  Doct: You see, her eyes are open.
  Gen: Ay, but their sense is shut [etc.]

19 The Three Witches [after 1783]
(Shakespeare, *Macbeth*, I, 3)

Oil on canvas, 75 × 90.2 cm
Exh: Birmingham 1949; Stratford-On-Avon
1956 (50): Bordeaux 1956 (58); Zurich 1969 (16)
Lit: Macandrew 1959 (60), p.40
Schiff: 734
*Stratford-upon-Avon, The Royal Shakespeare
Theatre, Picture Gallery and Museum*

The scene illustrated takes place on the heath.
  Banquo: . . . What are these,
  So wither'd and so wild in their attire,
  That look not like th'inhabitants o'the earth,
  And yet are on't? Live you? or are you aught
  That man may question? You seem to under-
    stand me,
  By each at once her choppy finger laying
  Upon her skinny lips: you should be women,
  And yet your beards forbid me to interpret
  That you are so.
  Macbeth: Speak, if you can: what are you?
  First Witch: All hail, Macbeth! hail to thee,
    Thane of Glamis!
  Sec. Witch: All hail, Macbeth! hail to thee,
    Thane of Cawdor!
  Third Witch: All hail Macbeth! that shalt
    be king hereafter.

20 The Witches Appear to Macbeth and Banquo
[1800–10]
(Shakespeare, *Macbeth*, I, 3)

Oil on canvas, 87 × 112 cm
Exh: Zurich 1969 (67)
Schiff: 1205
Riverside, California, Richard J. Carrott
(formerly Charles Alan, New York;
Mrs Windcatt, Torquay, Devon)

The subject is the same as that of No.19.

21   Garrick and Mrs Pritchard in Macbeth (1812)
(Shakespeare, *Macbeth*, II, 2)

Oil on canvas, 101 × 127 cm
Exh: London, Royal Academy, 1812; Inter-
national Exhibition, 1862 (270); R.E.A.
Wilson, 1935 (2); Roland, Browse & Delblanco,
1948 (2); London 1950 (25); *The Romantic
Movement*, 1959 (162); Zurich, 1969 (101)
Lit: Sitwell 1937, p.57; Sitwell 1943, repr.
after p.228; Woodward 1950, p.112; Antal
1956, p.143ff., note 6; Brion 1960, p.210,
repr. LX; Levey 1963, p.259, repr. in colour,
pl.457; Tomory 1972, pl.XI, p.124
Schiff: 1495
London, Tate Gallery, Inv. No.T733 (formerly
Clare Stanley-Clarke; T.E. Lowinsky)

Here Fuseli develops the drawing he made in 1760
after experiencing the scene on the stage (No.32).

The scene takes place immediately after the murder
by Macbeth of Duncan, King of Scotland, who was
staying with him in his castle in Inverness:

> *Lady Macbeth:* Go get some water,
> And wash this filthy witness from your hand.
> Why did you bring these daggers from the place?
> They must lie there: go carry them, and smear
> The sleepy grooms with blood.
> *Macbeth:* I'll go no more:
> I am afraid to think what I have done;
> Look on't again I dare not.
> *Lady Macbeth:* Infirm of purpose!
> Give me the daggers.

22   Mamillius in Charge of a Lady of the Court
[1785–6]
(Shakespeare, *The Winter's Tale*, II, 1)

Oil on canvas, diameter 43 cm
Exh: London, Roland, Browse & Delbanco,
1948; London, 1950; London, Burlington
House, *Winter Exhibition*, 1954 (5);
London, Agnew's, *Hampshire Pictures*, 1957;
Zurich 1969 (17) Lit: Woodward 1950, p.112.
Schiff: 744
Alresford, Hants., Ralph Dutton (formerly
Leger Galleries, London)

22

23

24

Fuseli's depiction departs considerably from the text in Shakespeare where the scene in fact takes place in a room in Leontes' palace. The 'faeries' may be stirred by the tale that Mamillius is about to recount:

> *Hermione:* And tell's a tale.
> *Mamillius:* Merry or sad shall't be?
> *Hermione:* As merry as you will.
> *Mamillius:* A sad tale's best for winter.
> I have one of sprites and goblins.
> *Hermione:* Let's have that, good sir.
> Come on, sit down: come on, and do your best
> To fright me with your sprites; . . .

23   Perdita [1785–6]
   (Shakespeare, *The Winter's Tale*, IV, 3)

   Oil on canvas, diameter 43 cm
   Exh: London, Roland, Browse & Delbanco,
   Paintings and Drawings by Henry Fuseli,
   1948; London 1950; London, Burlington
   House, *Winter Exhibition*, 1954 (5); London,
   Agnew's, *Hampshire Paintings*, 1957;
   Zurich 1969 (18)
   Lit: Woodward 1950, p.112
   Schiff: 745
   Alresford, Hants., Ralph Dutton (formerly
   Leger Galleries, London)

The inactivity of Fuseli's representation points to the reference to Perdita made by Time in his monologue at the opening of the act (IV, 1, 24ff.): 'Perdita, now grown in grace / Equal with wond'ring . . . ' The introduction of the fairies seems to have been suggested by the words of the old shepherd in the previous scene: 'This is fairy gold, boy, and 'twill prove so'. Fuseli turns into a reality the old shepherd's belief in the fairies' participation in Perdita's fate.

The painting actually shows her as described by Time and as she is seen by Prince Florizel (IV, 3):

> These your unusual weeds to each part of you
> Do give a life: no shepherdess, but Flora
> Peering in April's front . . .

24   Cobweb [1785–6]
   (Shakespeare, *A Midsummer Night's Dream*)

   Oil on canvas, diameter 45.7 cm
   Lit: Schiff 1961, p.10, repr. 3; Macandrew
   1959–60, p.34
   Schiff: 752
   London, Pierre Jeannerat (William Roscoe
   until 1816; Benjamin Hick, Bolton, until 1843)

In the centre Titania-Queen Mab leading on a chain the incubus (familiar from the various versions of 'The Nightmare'), a misshapen gnome with the features of an ape. According to Mercutio's description (*Romeo and Juliet*, I, 4), the fairy queen is not only the messenger of pleasant dreams but also 'the hag, when maids lie on their backs / That presses them and learns them first to bear . . . ' To Titania's right, Cobweb, with a feather as a broom. Right in front Mustard-seed, while Puck hovers above the scene.

25   Oberon Squeezes the Flower on Titania's Eyelids [1793–4]
(Shakespeare, *A Midsummer Night's Dream* II, 2)
Painting No.1 for 'Woodmason's Shakespeare Gallery'

Oil on canvas, 169 × 135 cm
Exh: Zurich 1926 (13); 1936 (29); 1941 (16); 1969 (32)
Schiff: 884
Wangen bei Olten, canton of Solothurn, Frau Melanie Kaufmann-Frey (formerly Galerie Bollag, Zurich)

Oberon determined to revenge himself on Titania for refusing to give him her changeling boy for his attendant, squeezes the juice of a magic flower on her eyelids, the effect of which will be that she will fall desperately in love with the first creature (animal or human) she sees when she wakes:

25

What thou seest when thou dost wake,
Do it for thy true-love take;
Love and languish for his sake:
Be it ounce, or cat, or bear,
Pard, or boar with bristled hair,
In thy eye that shall appear
When thou wak'st it is thy dear.
Wake when some vile thing is near.

26   Titania and Bottom [1780–90]
(Shakespeare, *A Midsummer Night's Dream*, IV, 1)
Painting No.2 for Boydell's 'Shakespeare Gallery'

Oil on canvas, 216 × 274 cm
Exh: London, British Institution, 1852 (144)
Repr: Engraving on copperplate with aquatint by J.P. Simon in 1796
Lit: Boydell 1793, X; Boydell 1802, XVIII; Forster 1789, p.130f.; Dayes 1805, p.327; Cunningham 1830, p.278; Haydon-Hazlitt 1838, p.213f.; Cunningham 1857, p.XC; Thornbury 1860, p.135; Timbs 1860, p.191; Dafforne 1861, p.327; Gurlitt 1900, p.55; Muther 1903, p.94, repr. p.93; Schmid 1904, I, p.55; Salaman-Holme 1916, repr. p.67; Pauli 1925, p.135, repr. p.480; Federmann 1927, pl.4, p.54; Denk 1930, p.127; Jaloux 1942, p.83ff.; Gradmann/Cetto 1944, p.73, repr. 63; Schiff 1961, p.12ff., repr. 4
Schiff: 753
London, Tate Gallery, Inv. No.1228. (In accordance with the wishes of her sister, the painting was presented to the National Gallery in 1887 by Miss Julia Carrick-Moore and was then transferred to the Tate Gallery in 1909.)

27

28

Titania, in the pose of Leonardo's *Leda*, calls on her fairies, who are dressed in contemporary styles, to attend to Bottom. Pease-blossom scratches his ass's head, Mustard-seed perches on his hand in order to assist Pease-blossom. Cobweb kills a bee and brings him the honey-bag. A buxom girl offers him a meal of 'dried pease'. The group with the young woman leading an old dwarf-like figure by a string is a symbol of the triumph of youth over old age, of the senses over the mind, of woman over man, along the lines of the saga of Merlin and Vyvyane. The hooded old woman on the right is holding a changeling just formed out of wax. The children in the group on the left are also artificial beings created by the witches. The small girl with the butterfly head is a variation of the type of child portrait created by Reynolds in which the girl's features resemble those of the cat, mouse or robin posed with her (*Felina, Muscipula, Robinetta*). The elves plunging into the calyx on the right correspond to a motif in Botticelli's illustration of Canto XXX of Dante's *Paradise*.

The lines illustrated are:
Titania: Come, sit thee down upon this flowery bed,
While I thy amiable cheeks do coy,
And stick musk-roses in thy sleek smooth head,
And kiss thy fair large ears, my gentle joy.

27 Titania Awakes, Surrounded by Attendant Fairies, Clinging Rapturously to Bottom, Still Wearing the Ass's Head [1793–4]
(Shakespeare, *A Midsummer Night's Dream* IV, 1)
Painting No.2 for 'Woodmason's Shakespeare Gallery'
Engraved by G. Rhodes

Oil on canvas, 169 × 135 cm
Exh: Zurich 1926 (13); 1936 (29); 1941 (17); London 1950 (11); Bremen/Dusseldorf 1957 (10); Zurich 1969 (33)
Lit: Knowles 1831, I, p.189; Salaman and Holmes 1916, repr. p.68; Federmann 1927, p.24; Beutler 1939, p.21; Gradmann/Cetto 1944, pl.63; Antal 1956, p.103ff.; Schiff 1961, p.21ff., repr. 12; Gaunt 1964, p.147, repr. 110; Tomory 1972, repr. 99, p.164.
Schiff: 885
Zurich, Kunsthaus

In the background on the left are two fairies as ladies of the court dressed in contemporary costume. Pease-blossom scratches Bottom on the head, while to the right Cobweb, in armour, is killing a bee on a thistle to obtain the honey-bag for Bottom. Round the group hovers a host of music-making and dancing fairies. According to Antal, the figure in the foreground with an insect's head was inspired by Callot's dancers in the *Commedia dell'Arte* series. Under the floating lute-player on the right there is an elf offering Bottom 'a handful or two of dried pease'. Above right, Puck can be seen surveying the scene. The elf dressed up as a jester is possibly Mustardseed.

28 Titania's Awakening [1785–9]
(Shakespeare, *A Midsummer Night's Dream*,
IV, 1)   (colour repr. p.21)
Painting No.3 for Boydell's 'Shakespeare
Gallery'

Oil on canvas, 222 × 280 cm
Exh: London, Boydell's Shakespeare Gallery,
1789ff.; Zurich 1969 (23)
Lit: Boydell 1802, XIX; Boydell 1803, Vol. I,
XXI; Forster 1789, p.130ff.; Dayes 1805,
p.327; Cunningham 1830, p.278; Haydon-
Hazlitt 1838, p.213ff.; Cunningham 1857,
p.XC; Thornbury 1860, p.135; Keller 1948;
Antal 1956, p.104; Schiff 1961, p.15ff., repr.
6–10; Irwin 1966, p.128; Tomory 1972, repr.
76, p.164
Repr: in an engraving by Thomas Ryder and
Thomas Ryder, Jun. 1803
Schiff: 754; cf. Nos. 25, 26, 27
Winterthur, Kunstmuseum (formerly Grete
Ring, Oxford)

Titania awakes and tells Oberon she dreamed she was in love with an ass. Oberon points to Bottom asleep beside her and orders Puck to remove the ass's head. The elf visible between Oberon and Titania symbolises the herb that destroyed the magic spell. To the left, a group of good fairies, at their feet the personification of laughter with a small bagpipe player. To the right – Fuseli's own invention – Bottom asleep surrounded by evil spirits. The incubus gallops over his forehead on his 'nightmare'. Three witches and their breed have lined up beside him. The one at the edge holds between her breasts the goblin born of her intercourse with the devil. At the same time she bends over her daughter born in wedlock whom she has initiated into the rites of witchcraft. The poor girl is evidently terrified by what she has learnt. Some minute fairies in the foreground are using Bottom's wooden clog as a boat to sail across a puddle.

29 Lady Constance, Arthur, Salisbury (1783)
(Shakespeare, *King John*, III, 1)

Oil on canvas, 63.5 × 53.3 cm
Exh: London, Royal Academy, 1783;
Cambridge, Mass., Harvard University, The
Fogg Museum of Art, *Sublimity and
Sensibility*, 1965 (9); Zurich 1969 (9)
Lit: La Farge 1953, p.32 with repr.; Tomory
1972, repr. 69, p.95
Schiff: 722

29

30

33

Northampton, Mass., The Smith College Museum of Art (presented by Eleanor Lamont Cunningham) (formerly Mark Oliver)

First version of this theme. In his last work (No.30) Fuseli considerably heightened the psychological implications of the scene.

Arthur is King John's nephew and Constance is Arthur's mother. They are in the King of France's tent with the Earl of Salisbury (standing right) who has been sent to call Constance to King John. He has told her of the marriage which has been arranged between Blanch of Spain, King John's niece, and Lewis the Dauphin, one that will thwart Constance's political ambitions for Arthur. She condemns the news of this alliance and refuses to see the King.

> *Constance:* I will not go with thee.
> I will instruct my sorrows to be proud;
> For grief is proud and makes his owner stoop.
> To me and to the state of my great grief
> Let kings assemble; for my grief's so great
> That no supporter but the huge firm earth
> Can hold it up: here I and sorrows sit;
> Here is my throne, bid kings come bow to it.

30 Lady Constance, Arthur, Salisbury (1825)
(Shakespeare, *King John*, III, 1)

Oil on canvas, 180 × 142 cm
Lit: Mason 1964, p.101
Schiff: 1814; cf. No.29
Zurich, Bruno Meissner (formerly C. Margiotta)

Fuseli died before he could complete this painting. It was painted for James Carrick Moore and is a further development of the version of the same theme executed in 1783 (No.29).

31 Cardinal Beaufort Terrified by the Ghost of Gloucester (1808)
(Shakespeare, *King Henry VI*, Part 2, III, 3)

Oil on canvas, 114 × 143 cm
Exh: London, Royal Academy, 1808
Schiff: 1787
London, Sabin Galleries Ltd

31

The Duke of Gloucester has been murdered by the Duke of Suffolk and Cardinal Beaufort. The Duke of Suffolk has been banished and Cardinal Beaufort has suddenly been taken ill. He lies dying, haunted by the ghost of Gloucester:

> I'll give a thousand pound to look upon him.
> He hath no eyes, the dust has blinded them.
> Comb down his hair; look! look! it stands upright,
> Like lime-twigs set to catch my winged soul . . .

32 **Garrick and Mrs Pritchard as Macbeth and
Lady Macbeth after the Murder of Duncan**
[*c*.1766]
(Shakespeare, *Macbeth*, II, 2)
Engraved in 1804 by J. Heath

Watercolour heightened with white,
32.3 × 29.4 cm
Inscr. bottom left: 'H.F.'; on the floor the
inscription: 'My husband . . . I've done the
deed'
Exh: Zurich 1969 (122)
Lit: Knowles 1831, I, p.40; Federmann 1927,
p.35; Woodward 1950, p.112; Antal 1956,
p.18ff., 143, note 6; Mason 1964, repr. 5;
Dotson 1965, p.52, repr. 19; Tomory 1972,
p.70, 124, repr. 160
Schiff: 341, cf. No.21
Zurich, Kunsthaus, Inv. No.1938/650
(Ganz Bequest)

34

33 **Macbeth and the Armed Head** [*c*.1774]
(Shakespeare, *Macbeth*, IV, 1)

Pen and ink with reddish-brown wash,
25.2 × 38.6 cm
Lit: Todd 1946, repr. 19; Powell 1951, p.15;
Mason 1964, p.98, repr. 7

35

Schiff: 457a
London, Trustees of the British Museum,
Roman Album, Fol. 8v, No.10, Inv.
No.1885-3-14-208

The scene takes place in a cavern in the middle of which is a boiling cauldron. Macbeth has come to find out his destiny from the witches. The first apparition is an armed head who warns:
   Macbeth! Macbeth! Macbeth! beware Macduff;
   Beware the Thane of Fife.

34   The Witches Show Macbeth Banquo's Descendants 1773–9
Shakespeare, *Macbeth*, IV, 1)

Pen and ink and wash, 36.0 × 42.0 cm
Inscr. bottom centre in his own hand with black chalk '73 R'; beside it in paint 'Z. Feb. 79'
Exh: Zurich 1926 (137); 1941 (152); London 1950 (43); New York 1954 (2); Bremen/ Dusseldorf 1957 (61); Zurich 1969 (144)
Lit: Federmann 1927 pl.44 top; Blunt 1959, p.20 pl.11c; Antal 1962, p.180; Dotson 1965, repr. 4.
Schiff: 458
Zurich, Kunsthaus, Inv. No.1916/17

The figure of Macbeth is compiled from motifs from the Dioscuri on the Monte Cavallo. The more simplified drawing of the ghosts points to the influence of Luca Cambiaso of whom Fuseli possessed numerous drawings. The composition itself appears to have been completed in 1773; in 1779 he merely added more wash to it in Zurich.

The scene follows on from that of No.33. This is the last vision shown to Macbeth by the witches, in which Banquo's descendants appear as the eight future kings, the last carrying a looking glass.

35   Lady Macbeth Sleepwalking 1798
(Shakespeare, *Macbeth*, V, 1)

Pen and ink wash, 30.5 × 18.0 cm
Inscr. on one of the steps: 'Septr. 98'; on the back: *The Murder of Banquo*
Lit: Powell 1951, 45; Witt Collection 1956, p.20
Schiff: 1014
London, Courtauld Institute of Art (Witt Collection), Inv. No.2156

The same subject as No.18.

36

36a

36   The King of Denmark is Poisoned by his Brother While Sleeping 1771
(Shakespeare, *Hamlet*, I, 5, 58–78)

Pen and ink and wash over pencil, 43.6 × 59.6 cm
Inscr. bottom right: 'Roma 71 Oct.'
Exh: Zurich 1969 (142)
Lit: Schiff 1959, 9

37

Schiff: 445
Zurich, Graphische Sammlung der
Eidgenössischen Technischen Hochschule

The composition is based on a red-figured vase (36a)
painting attributed by Beazley to the Berlin Dinos
painter (Att. Redfig. vas. 2, 2, 1154, No.35; British
Museum, F.65) which is illustrated in Vol. II, pl.32,
of d'Hancarville's *Antiquités Etrusques, Grecques et*
Romaines, Tirées du Cabinet de M. Hamilton,
Naples 1766–7: Pederastic scene with spectators.
The action is presented in the form of an allegory.
In his first monologue Hamlet says of his father:
(I, 2)

So excellent a king: that was to this
Hyperion to a satyr

(Reference by Andreas Rumpf)
The connection of the scene depicted with this
mythological metaphor explains the 'ideal' nudity of
the figures as well as the otherwise inexplicable fact
that the elderly king should have such a youthful
appearance. He is presented as Hyperion-Helios,
and his murderer as a satyr. Fuseli has generalised
the murder of the king, making it into an allegory
of the destruction of a light principle by a dark,
instinctual one.

The ghost of Hamlet's father describes his murder:
. . . Sleeping within mine orchard,
My custom always in the afternoon,
Upon my secure hour thy uncle stole,
With juice of cursed hebona in a vial,
And in the porches of mine ears did pour
The leperous distilment . . . .

38

37   Hamlet visits Ophelia in her Closet [1810–15]
(Shakespeare, *Hamlet*, II, 1)

Pen and grey wash, 40.5 × 32.0 cm
Inscr. bottom right: '82'; on the reverse
collection stamp: 'G.K.S' Watermark 'J.
Bigg 1799'
Exh: Zurich, 1926 (296); 1941 (437); 50 *Jahre*
Gottfried Keller-Stiftung, Berne 1942 (250);
Zurich 1969 (278)
Schiff: 1544
Zurich, Kunsthaus, Inv. No.1940/196 (on loan
from the Gottfried Keller Foundation)

The drawing illustrates Hamlet's visit to Ophelia as
she describes it to Polonius. (Hamlet had just seen
the ghost of his father who recounted his murder by
his brother, Hamlet's uncle). She says Hamlet
arrived in disarray, 'no hat upon his head' looking
fraught and pale:

He took me by the wrist and held me hard,
Then goes he to the length of all his arm,
And, with his other hand thus o'er his brow,
He falls to such perusal of my face
As he would draw it.

Subject identified by Bjarne Jörnäs.

39

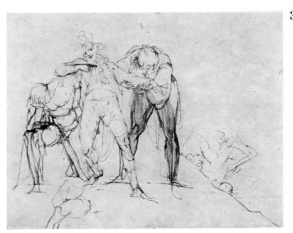

40r   40v

41

42

38   Lear and the Dead Cordelia 1774
(Shakespeare, *King Lear*, V, 3)

Pen and ink and yellowish wash,
38.0 × 31.0 cm
Inscr. in sepia at bottom left: 'Lear'; at
bottom right '35'; and in ink: 'Roma 74 may'
Exh: Zurich 1926 (107); 1941 (237); London
1950 (41); New York 1954 (27); Bremen/
Dusseldorf 1957 (63)
Lit: Federmann 1927, p.40; Ganz 1947, p.21;
Lankheit 1951, p.179; Antal 1956, p.34, 39
Schiff: 465
Zurich, Kunsthaus, Inv. No.1914/25

The scene is the British camp near Dover. Lear and
Cordelia have been imprisoned, and in spite of Edmund's last minute attempt to reprieve her Cordelia has been killed. Lear holds Cordelia in his
arms saying:

A plague upon you, murderers, traitors all!
I might have sav'd her; now, she's gone for ever!

**39   The Mad Lear, Supported by Edgar and
Gloucester, is Discovered by Cordelia's Envoy**
[*c*.1800–10]
(Shakespeare, *King Lear*, IV, 6)

Pen and ink over pencil, with some wash,
23.1 × 31.0 cm
Outlines of the drawing visible on the reverse
Exh: Zurich 1926 (190); 1941 (392)
Schiff: 1409
Zurich, Kunsthaus, Inv. No.1940/20 (formerly
Paul Hürlimann and Arnold Otto Meyer,
Hamburg)

The scene takes place in the country near Dover.
Gloucester and Edgar have met Lear, bedecked with
flowers and, by this time, mad. The drawing illustrates the reaction of Cordelia's envoy on finding
him:

A sight most pitiful in the meanest wretch,
Past speaking of in a King!

40   Balcony Scene 1815
(Shakespeare, *Romeo and Juliet*, III, 5)

Pencil, 27.0 × 18.0 cm
Inscr. (covered by the mount): 'P.H. 10
April 1815'; Watermark: 'Golding &
Snelgrove 1814'; on the back, another study for
the same subject.
Lit: Powell 1951, 53a
Schiff: 1552/1553
London, Private collection

Romeo has been banished after killing Mercutio,
but with the help of Juliet's nurse and Friar Lau-
rence, he climbed at night up to Juliet's room.
   The drawing shows Romeo leaving at dawn to
make his way to Mantua,

43

44

41 Ariel Driving in Trinculo, Stephano and Caliban 1774
(Shakespeare, *The Tempest*, V, 1)

Pen and ink and wash, 36.0 × 47.3 cm
Inscr. at bottom left: 'Tempest'; at bottom
right: 'Roma april 74'
Lit: Federmann 1927, pl.59 at bottom;
Oppel 1965, p.96, pl.17
Schiff: 467
London, Private collection

Prospero is to end his powers of magic and free
Ariel. But first Ariel must gather together those
whom Prospero shipwrecked on the island and has
since held under his charms. Trinculo, the court jester, and Stephano, a drunken butler, have met up
with Prospero's monstrous slave, Caliban. They are
drunk and have been plotting to kill Prospero. Here
Ariel drives them in to join the others.

42 Rosalind and Celia Watch Orlando Wrestle with Charles [1777]
(Shakespeare, *As You Like It*, I, 2)

Pen and ink, 27.5 × 17.5 cm
Inscr. at bottom: 'R. May 77'; on the right a
sketch of a similar female figure
Lit: Ganz 1947, p.24; Saxl and Wittkower
1947, 83.3; Woodward 1950, p.360; Antal
1956, p.38ff.
Schiff: 469
London, Victoria and Albert Museum,
Dyce Collection 777

The old Duke has been banished by his younger brother, Frederick. Rosalind, the old Duke's daughter,
has stayed at court with Frederick's daughter,
Celia. They are watching Orlando wrestle with
Charles, the court wrestler, who has a formidable
reputation.
Ros: O excellent young man!
Celia: If I had a thunderbolt in mine eye, I can
tell who should down.

43 Garrick as Duke of Gloucester Waiting for Lady Anne at the Funeral Procession of her Father-in-law, King Henry VI [1766]
(Shakespeare, *King Richard III*, I, 2)

Pen and wash, with pencil and heightened
with white, 31.7 × 45.7 cm
Inscr. at bottom right: 'H.F. 1766'; on the
base of the pillar: 'ANNA HENRI. VIi
RELIQUIAS EFFERENS
A RICHARDO SOCERI MARITIQUE
INTERFECTORE EXCIPITUR
QUEMQUE DIRIS MOX
DEVOVERAT EI SE CONNUBIO
FINGIT'
Exh: Zurich 1941 (215); 1969 (121)
Lit: Knowles 1931, I, p.40; Federmann 1927,
p.35; Fischer 1942, p.8ff., repr. 2; Ganz 1947,
p.5; Antal 1956, p.18; Mason 1964, p.94 and
repr. 4; Oppel 1965, p.101, repr. 49; Tomory
1972, pp.69, 71ff., 163, repr. 12
Schiff: 340
Zurich, Kunsthaus, Inv. No.1938/657 (Ganz
Bequest; formerly Alderman Cadell; Countess
of Guilford)

The scene illustrated takes place in a London street.
Gloucester, the future Richard III, murderer of
King Henry VI and his son Edward, is waiting for
Edward's widow, Lady Anne, whom even so he in-
tends to make his wife. The lines illustrated, spoken
by Lady Anne, are as follows:
Set down, set down your honourable load,
If honour may be shrouded in a hearse,
Whilst I a while obsequiously lament
The untimely fall of virtuous Lancaster.

44 Richard III Sees the Ghosts of his Victims 1777
(Shakespeare, *King Richard III*, V, 3)

Pen and ink and wash, 30.4 × 48.0 cm
Inscr. bottom left: 'da Fusely Roma 1777'
Lit: Federmann 1927, p.40, 47; Powell 1951,
p.9; Hofmann 1952, p.172; Antal 1956, p.47ff,
and passim
Schiff: 444
London, Trustees of the British Museum,
Roman Album, fol.59v, No.78, Inv. No.
1885-2-14-270

Richard III, when attempting to win the crown,
had to murder many important figures who stood in
his way. Here their ghosts file past him as he dreams.
Ghost of Lady Anne: Richard, thy wife,
that wretched Anne thy wife,
That never slept a quiet hour with thee,
Now fills thy sleep with perturbations:
To-morrow in the battle think on me,
And fall thy edgeless sword: despair, and die!

45 Falstaff and Doll 1771
(Shakespeare, *King Henry IV*, Part 2; II, 4)

Pen and ink and wash, 26.0 × 22.0 cm
Inscr. at bottom in pencil: 'Roma 71'
Exh: Zurich 1926 (101); 1941 (225)
Schiff: 435
Zurich, Kunsthaus, Inv. No.1940/51 (from the
Arnold Otto Meyer collection, Hamburg)

The scene takes place in a room in the Boar's Head
Tavern, Eastcheap. The Prince and Poins who are
both disguised as tapsters are behind Falstaff and
Doll Tearsheet.
Fal: Thou dost give me flattering busses.
Dol: By my troth, I kiss thee with a most
constant heart.
Fal: I am old, I am old.
Dol: I love thee better than I love e'er a scurvy
young boy of them all.

**46 The Captured Duke of York is Crowned by
Queen Margaret with a Paper Crown** [1772]
(Shakespeare, *King Henry VI*, Part 3, I, 4)

Pen and sepia wash, 44.0 × 48.5 cm
Falsely signed: 'Blake'
Schiff: 441; cf. No.47
Chapel Hill, The University of North Carolina,
The William Hayes Ackland Memorial Art
Center (formerly Richard Lee Feigen and
Peter H. Deitsch, New York)

45

Fuseli cannot have seen *Henry VI* during his first
stay in London because during that period it was
dropped from the repertory (cf. Charles Beecher
Hogan, *Shakespeare in the Theatre, 1701–1800, II,
A Record of Performances in London 1751–1800,*
Oxford 1957). Beside Clifford he arbitrarily includes
the figure of a jester who holds a fool's cap ready
for the humiliated rebel.

This episode takes place during one of the battles
for the crown of England between the House of
Lancaster under King Henry VI and the House of
York under the Duke. The Duke of York has just
been taken prisoner and Queen Margaret is mock-
ing him.

Ay, marry Sir, now looks he like a King!
Ay, this is he that took King Henry's chair;
And this is he was his adopted heir.

46

**47 Queen Margaret Places a Paper Crown on the
Head of the Captured Duke of York** [1800–10]
(Shakespeare, *King Henry VI*, Part 3, I, 4)

Black chalk, 22.1 × 21.9 cm
Inscr. in an unknown hand: 'Gretchen and
her brother, Goethe'; collection stamp of the
Countess of Guilford; on the reverse fragments
of a head, shoulder, hand, and a sketch of a
woman's hand
Lit: Ganz 1947, 89
Schiff: 1406
Basle, Öffentliche Kunstsammlung, Inv.
No.1914.132.18

Hastily executed repetition of composition No.46.
The main difference is that in that work York still
attempts in vain to free himself, whereas here he is
depicted already sinking back exhausted. Fuseli has
also abandoned the figure of the man who is trying
to put the fool's cap on York's head.

47

**48 Arthur, Duke of Brittany, Begs Hubert de
Burgh Not to Have his Eyes Burnt Out** [1775]
(Shakespeare, *King John*, IV, 1)

Pen and ink and wash, 25.2 × 38.2 cm.
The sheet is torn and now consists of four
pieces stuck together
Schiff: 433
London, Trustees of the British Museum,
Roman Album, fol.20v, No.24, Inv.
No.1885-3-14-222

Hubert de Burgh has been commanded to burn out Arthur's eyes with hot irons. Arthur beseeches Hubert to show mercy. Fuseli illustrates the following lines:

O! save me, Hubert, save me! my eyes are out
Even with the fierce looks of these bloody men.

49 Queen Katherine's Dream [1781–3]
(Shakespeare, *King Henry VIII*, IV, 2)

Engraving by F. Bartolozzi after a lost painting by Fuseli, 45.7 × 35.5 cm
Lit: Antal 1956, p.85, pl.31a; Boase 1963, p.153, pl.20c
Schiff: 729
London, Trustees of the British Museum

This engraving was made after Fuseli's contribution to Thomas Macklin's never completed *Poets' Gallery*. It was published on 4 April 1783. In the Victoria and Albert Museum there are two fragments of another version of the same theme (Schiff 730a and b) which are probably identical with the painting of *Queen Katherine's Dream* exhibited at the Royal Academy in 1781. Fuseli's treatment of the genii who appear to the Queen the night before her execution indicate his love of the ballet and theatre.

Katherine, now divorced from King Henry, is unwell. She dreams that an ethereal troop, dressed in white with garlands on their heads, dances and pays reverence to her.

DESIGNS FOR SHAKESPEARE FRESCOES

50 Twelfth Night [1777–8]

Left: nothing
Centre: top: Olivia, behind her, Amor; Inscr. on a tablet: VIOLA (Fuseli's mistake, Viola appears in men's clothes throughout the play); Bottom: Amor
Right: Maria and the clown peeping through a window at the imprisoned Malvolio (IV, 2)

Pen and ink and wash, 35.5 × 20.8 cm
Lit: Mason 1964, p.85; Schiff 1964, p.130, repr. 82; Tomory 1972, repr. 33, p.72, 80ff
Schiff: 475
London, Trustees of the British Museum,
Roman Album, fol. 48v, No.67, Inv. No.1885-3-14-259

This and the following three drawings belong to a bold project conceived by Fuseli at the end of his stay in Rome. It consisted of a room decorated with frescoed scenes from Shakespeare's dramas incorporated into an architectonic construction imitating the Sistine ceiling. It was to be dedicated to Shakespeare's genius. The four surviving sketches are probably only a fraction of what Fuseli in fact executed. There was presumably no possibility of realising the project. A detailed examination of the

51

52

53

four designs even proves that Fuseli had no clear idea of the overall architectonic system. Each design consists of two halved lunette shapes separated by a spandrel. In the designs for *Macbeth* and *The Tempest* this system is subdivided horizontally. Whereas these are scarcely more than a conglomeration of individual motifs, the designs for *Twelfth Night* and *King Lear* do attempt some unification. Iconographically each of these subdivided designs form a single unit with the most important scenes from the play in question grouped round the protagonist; formally, however, they are fragments. The halved lunette shapes demand to be completed. The various frescoes could only be connected if a window or pilaster were inserted between them. However this would separate the often abruptly severed illustrations of the various plays, and would also destroy the decorative unity of the surface area.

Despite their fragmentary character, the drawings are of immense historical importance. The idea of re-interpreting the concept of the Sistine Chapel (one of the noblest places of worship in Christendom) as a memorial to a poet seems an audacious way of paying homage to genius.

Fuseli's designs are not so much a secularisation of Michelangelo's representation of 'Theocracy or the empire of religion' (Fuseli, Lecture III) as a deification of the poet. In this sense he anticipates the Romantic conception of the artist as autonomous creator almost on a level with god. In his maturity Fuseli rejected outright any such mixture or interchange of the functions of religion and art; only his admiration for Shakespeare could cause him to break down these barriers.

51 Macbeth [1777–8]

Left-hand lunette: top: The murder of Banquo (III, 3); bottom: Lady Macbeth sleepwalking (V, 1)
Spandrel: top: Macbeth and the Witches; Inscr: 'Macbeth'; bottom: Macduff, Lady Macduff and their son (IV, 2)
Right-hand lunette: top: the murder of Duncan

(II, 2); bottom: the three witches

Pen and ink and brown wash, 27.3 × 19.6 cm
Lit: Powell 1951, No.10; Mason 1964, p.85, pl.1; Schiff 1964, p.130, repr. 84, p.80ff.
Schiff: 476
London, Trustees of the British Museum, Roman Album, fol.46v, No.65, Inv. No.1885-3-14-257

52 The Tempest [1777–8]

Left-hand lunette: top: Trinculo and Stephano bent over Caliban (II, 2); bottom: Ferdinand and Miranda (III, 1).
Spandrel: top: Prospero and Ariel; Inscr. on a plaque in the centre: 'PROSPERO'; bottom: Ariel confined in the cloven pine by the witch Sycorax (I, 2).
Right-hand lunette: top: The ship-wrecked sailors leap overboard, protected by Ariel's spell (I, 2); bottom: Caliban dragging a tree trunk (II, 2)

Pen and ink and brown wash, 27.2 × 19.7 cm
Lit: Mason 1964, p.85, pl.1; Schiff 1964, p.130, repr. 84; Tomory, repr. 35, p.80 ff.
Schiff: 477
London, Trustees of the British Museum, Roman Album, fol.45v, No.64, Inv. No.1885-3-14-256

53 King Lear [1777–8]

Left-hand lunette: Edgar
Spandrel: top: Lear with the dead Cordelia (V, 3); no inscription on the plaque; bottom: Goneril.
Right-hand lunette: Lear in the Cornfield (V, 2)

Pen and ink and brown wash, 27.2 × 19.7 cm
Lit: Mason 1964, p.85, pl.1; Schiff 1964, p.130, repr. 85; Irwin 1966, repr. 123; Tomory 1972, repr. 32, p.80ff
Schiff: 478
London, Trustees of the British Museum, fol.47v, No.66, Inv. No.1885-3-14-258

The Classics

54

58

54 Dido on the Funeral Pyre (1781)
(Virgil, *Aeneid*, IV, 688-705)

Oil on canvas, 243 × 183 cm
Exh: London, Royal Academy, 1781; Zurich,
1913 (54); 1941 (7)
Lit: Cunningham 1830, p.279; Thornbury
1860, p.135; Federmann 1927, p.51, 169;
Tomory 1972, p.33
Schiff: 713
New York, Richard L. Feigen & Co.

Dido sinks back dying, Aeneas' sword beside her.
Her sister Anna crouches at her feet. Iris appears in
the clouds above and cuts off Dido's hair. On the
left is a large gold oil jar.

55 Theseus Receiving the Thread from Ariadne
(1788)
(Ovid, *Metamorphoses*, VIII, 172-3)

Oil on canvas, 96 × 73 cm
Exh: London, Royal Academy, 1788; London,
Suffolk Street, 1833 (12); Manchester, *Art
Treasures Exhibition*, 1857 (105); Zurich 1913
(55); 1926 (11); 1941 (8); Bremen/Dusseldorf
1957 (11); Zurich, 1969 (4)
Lit: Meyer 1805, p.297, note 1; Horner 1826,
p.10; Anon. 1826, p.110; Fuseli 1842, p.164;
Federmann 1927, p.54ff., pl.13; Jaloux 1942,
p.165; Antal 1956, p.91; Macandrew 1959/60,
p.7, 21, 43.
Schiff: 714
Zurich, Kunsthaus

The group is based on the relief of *Perseus and Andromeda* in the Capitoline Museum, Rome, which
Fuseli sketched there in 1778 (Nationalmuseum
Stockholm; Schiff 661; cf. No.79). Fuseli links the
figures together in an ornamental way reminiscent
of Bartholomäus Spranger's mythological paintings.

Minos imprisoned the monster, half bull half man,
offspring of his wife Pasiphaë and Poseidon's bull
(see cat No.83) in a maze specially constructed for
him by Daedalus. On two occasions victims were
thrown to him to feast on but on the third, one of
the victims was Theseus who managed to escape
with the help of Ariadne. She gave him a thread to
mark the route through the maze and by rewinding
this Theseus was able to retrace his steps and find
the doorway that had eluded his predecessors.

**56 Venus Persuades Cupid to Fill Psyche with
Love for the Lowest Mortal** [1795–1800]
(Apuleius, *Metamorphoses*, IV, 31)

Oil on canvas, 71.5 × 82.5 cm
Exh: Zurich 1941 (70), pl.XVII; 1969 (29)

Schiff: 878

Winterthur, Kunstmuseum (donated by the Galerieverein in 1941)

The group of Venus and Cupid is representative of the many instances in classical literature where the goddess tenderly persuades her son to strike someone with his arrows. The third figure can only be interpreted as a companion of Venus. Parallel situations can be found in Ovid, *Metamorphoses V* (363ff.) where Venus persuades Cupid to make Pluto fall in love with Proserpina; Nonnos, *Dionysiaka* (33, 143ff.) where Aphrodite persuades Eros to fill Morpheus with love for Chalcomede; and (41, 399) Aphrodite persuades Eros to make both Poseidon and Dionysus fall in love simultaneously with Beroe, her daughter by Adonis.

57 Sleep and Death Bear the Corpse of Sarpedon Away to Lycia (1803)
(Homer, *Iliad*, XVI, 679ff.)
Engraved by J. Stow in the translations of Homer by Pope (London 1805) and Cowper (London 1810)

Oil on canvas, 91.4 × 71 cm
Exh: London, Royal Academy, 1811; Liverpool, Academy, 1812 (184); Zurich 1969 (58)
Schiff: 1190
Zurich, Haus zum Rechberg

The composition combines allusions to the iconographic type of the 'Throne of Grace in the clouds' with a reminiscence of Poussin's 'Vision of St. Paul' of 1650 (cf. Walter Friedlaender, *Nicolas Poussin*, Munich 1914, repr. 238).

Sarpedon has been killed by Patroclus; Zeus has asked Apollo to carry his body off to Lycia. The painting illustrates the lines:

> Forthwith then he [Apollo] lifted up goodly Sarpedon forth from out the range of darts, and when he had borne him far away, bathed him in the streams of the river, and anointed him with ambrosia, and clothed him about with immortal raiment, and gave him to swift conveyers to bear with them, even to the brethren, Sleep and Death, who set him speedily in the rich land of wide Lycia (A. T. Murray).

58 Thetis Asks Hephaestus, Supported on Two Artificial Golden Virgins, for Weapons for Achilles (1803)
(Homer, *Iliad*, XVIII, 410ff.)
Engraved by E. Smith in the translations of Homer by Pope (1805) and Cowper (1810)

Oil on canvas, 91 × 71 cm
Exh: Liverpool, Academy, 1812 (185); Zurich 1926 (36); 1941 (59); Paris 1948 (119); Geneva 1948 (203); London 1950 (22); Bremen/ Dusseldorf 1957 (31); Zurich 1969 (59).
Lit: Federmann 1927, p.64
Schiff: 1191
Zurich, Kunsthaus (formerly Paul Hürlimann)

55

56

57

Thetis has come to the palace of Hephaestus to ask him to make some armour for Achilles to wear in his fight with the Trojans. The painting shows Thetis seated with Charis, Hephaestus' wife, beside her. The lines illustrated are:

> . . . but there moved swiftly to support their lord handmaidens wrought of gold in the semblance of living maids. In them is understanding in their hearts, and in them speech and strength, and they know cunning handiwork by gift of the immortal gods. These busily moved to support their lord, and he, limping nigh to where Thetis was . . . (A. T. Murray).

59 Achilles Grasps at the Shade of Patroclus
(1803)
(Homer, *Iliad*, XXIII, 99ff.)
Engraved by J. Heath in the translations of Homer by Pope (London 1805) and Cowper (London 1810)

Oil on canvas, 91 × 71 cm
Exh: Liverpool, Academy, 1812 (12); Zurich 1969 (60)
Lit: Federmann 1927, p.64; Antal 1956, p.97; Tomory 1972, repr. 248, p.120
Schiff: 1192; cf. No.66
Zurich, Kunsthaus (formerly Paul Hürlimann)

Patroclus appeared to Achilles in his sleep and begged him to bury his body instantly so that he might pass through the Gates of Hades. He warned Achilles that he was to share the same destiny and asked that they should be buried together. The painting illustrates:

> Then in answer spake to him Achilles, swift to foot: 'Wherefore O head beloved, art thou come hither, and thus givest me charge about each thing? Nay, verily, I will fulfil thee all, and will hearken even as thou biddest. But I pray thee, draw thou nigher; though it be but for a little space let us clasp our arms one about the other, and take our fill of dire lamenting'.
> So saying he reached forth with his hands . . . (A. T. Murray).

60 The Blinded Polyphemus, at the Entrance to his Cave, Strokes the Ram under which Odysseus Lies Concealed (1803)
(Homer, *Odyssey*, IX, 440ff.)
Engraved by I.G. Walker in the translations of Homer by Pope (London 1805) and Cowper (London 1810)

Oil on canvas, 91 × 71 cm
Exh: Zurich 1969 (61)
Lit: Federmann 1927, p.64ff., with repr.
Antal 1956, p.97, 113, note 82; Schrade 1931, p.14, 24; Beutler, p.22; Gradmann/Cetto 1944, p.75, repr. 67.
Schiff: 1194
Zurich, Private collection

Odysseus and his men crossed to the land of the Cyclopes, where they were taken captive by Polyphemus and imprisoned in his cave. They drove a pole into his eye while he was sleeping, and planned to escape by hiding themselves under his sheep. At dawn the sheep began to move to pasture, carrying the men with them. The lines illustrated are:

> And their master, distressed with grievous pains, felt along the backs of all the sheep as they stood up before him, but in his folly he marked not this, that my men were bound beneath the breasts of his fleecy sheep. Last of all the flock the ram went forth, burdened with the weight of his fleece and my cunning self. (A. T. Murray).

61 The Erinyes Drive Alcmaeon from the Corpse of his Mother, Eriphyle, Whom He Has Killed
(1821)

Oil on canvas, 122 × 157 cm
Exh: London, Royal Academy, 1821; Zurich 1926 (49); 1936 (43); 1941 (64); Geneva 1948 (209); Ostend 1953 (13); London 1959 (161); Zurich 1969 (96)
Schiff: 1489
Zurich, Kunsthaus (formerly F. Girtanner, Zurich)

In the catalogue of the Royal Academy exhibition in 1821 Fuseli himself gave the following elucidation of this picture:

> Amphiaros, a chief of the Argolic league against Thebes, endowed with prescience, to avoid his fate, withdrew to a secret place known only to Eriphyle his wife, which she, seduced by the presents of Polynices, disclosed: thus betrayed, he on departing, commanded Alcmaeon his son, on being informed of his death, to destroy his mother. Eriphyle fell by the hand of her son, who fled, pursued by her avenging Furies.

Above the dead Eriphyle are the three Furies, the foremost of whom turns back towards her companions. They point towards Alcmaeon whose face, distorted with pain, can just be seen at the extreme left of the picture which has darkened considerably with age.

Fuseli does not indicate his source for this motif, of which there are several versions. Furthermore, none of these versions corresponds exactly to his description. He probably combined motifs from Hyginus (*Fables*, 73) and Statius (*Thebais*, IV, 187ff.). In one important respect, however, he departs totally from tradition. Wherever the jewelry which tempts Eriphyle to betray her husband is mentioned specifically, it is referred to as a necklace, not a bracelet. In the *Canterbury Tales*, on the other hand, the Wife of Bath refers to 'Amphiorax' having received 'an ouche of gold'. The jewelry Fuseli chooses for his Eriphyle is none other than a large gold brooch (ouche) attached to a bracelet. For the pose of the dead Eriphyle he took as his model the figure of the dead Clytaemnestra on Orestes Sarcophagi (e.g. the example in the Galleria dei Candelabri in the Vatican, reproduced in *Admiranda Bartoli*, Rome 1960, repr. 52.)

62 Autolycus Names his Grandson Odysseus in the Presence of his Parents and the Nurse Eurycleia [1765–9]
(Homer, *Odyssey*, XIX, 399ff.)

Pen and sepia wash heightened with gouache, 51 × 67 cm
Inscr. on the pedestal two lines from the *Odyssey*, XIX, 407–409: 'Lo, inasmuch as I am come hither as one that has been angered with many, both men and women, over the fruitful earth, therefore let the name by which the child is named be Odysseus.' (A. T. Murray)
Exh: Zurich 1926 (108); 1941 (220); Bremen/ Dusseldorf 1957 (54); Zurich 1969 (116)
Lit: Ganz 1947, 8; Hofmann 1952, p.170
Schiff: 324
Zurich, Kunsthaus, Inv. No.1938/220
(Ganz donation)

59

63 Teiresias Drinks the Sacrificial Blood
[1774–8]
(Homer, *Odyssey*, XI, 96)

Pen and ink and wash, 35.0 × 47.9 cm
Schiff: 387
London, British Museum, Roman Album, fol.53v., No.72, Inv. No.1885-3-14-264

In his illustration of the invocation of the spirits, the climax of Odysseus' journey to Hades, Fuseli depicts the blind prophet Teiresias in the sacrificial trench performing the ritual of drinking the blood with an eagerness that is positively barbaric. Odysseus stands behind the trench holding the souls back with his sword. His figure is based on the Hellenistic statue of a Niobid in the Uffizi (cf. W. Amelung, *Führer durch die Antiken in Florenz*, Munich 1897, No.181).

60

64 Thetis Mourning the Body of Achilles 1780
(Homer, *Odyssey*, XXIV, 47)

Ink and grey wash, 41.8 × 55.8 cm
Inscr. bottom right in pencil: 'London apr. 80'; bottom left: πολλος τις γαρ εκειτο παρηορος ενθα και ενθα
(Nestor fighting with Ereuthalion, Homer, *Iliad*, VII, 156): κειτομεγας μεγαλωστι λελασμενος ἱπποσυναων
(Agamemnon with Achilles in Hades, Homer, *Odyssey*, XXIV, 40); at the right edge: τρεχω δε χερσιν οὐ ποδωκιᾳ Σκελων
(The Pythian Prophetess leaving the Temple of Apollo, Aeschylus, *Eumenides* 37)
Exh: The University of Chicago, *An Exhibition of Drawings and Prints by English Artists*

61

62

63

64

65

of the Eighteenth and Early Nineteenth
Centuries, 1946 (16); Cambridge, Mass.,
Harvard University, The Fogg Museum of Art,
Sublimity and Sensibility, April 1965 (10)
Lit: Ganz 1947, 70; Lankheit 1951, p.178
Schiff: 799a
Chicago, Art Institute, Leonora Hall Gurley
Collection, Inv. No.2221/54

The quotations are as follows: 'as a huge sprawling
bulk he lay stretched this way and that . . . ' (A.T.
Murray) 'and thou in the whirl of dust didst lie
mighty in thy mightiness, forgetful of thy horse-
manship' (A.T. Murray) 'I run with the aid of my
hands, not with any nimbleness of limb . . . ' (H.W.
Smyth). The meaning of the strange configuration
in the sky resembling a rower with flowing hair is
obscure. A similar element occurs in a drawing in
Auckland (Schiff 1804).

65 The Daughters of Pandareus [c.1795]
   (Homer, *Odyssey*, XX, 60–78)

Pen and ink and wash, heightened with white,
52 × 63 cm
Inscr. bottom right: ΠΑΝΔΑΡΕΗ
On the back: left, a pencil study of a seated
woman; right, sketch of a head
Exh: Zurich 1969 (185)
Lit: Ganz 1947
Schiff: 984
Zurich, Kunsthaus, Inv. No.1940/142
(formerly Paul Hürlimann)

In Greek mythology Pandareus stole the golden
mastiff which guarded the Temple of Zeus on Crete.
To escape punishment, he fled with his family to
Sicily, where he and his wife were killed by Zeus.
Their daughters, however, were taken care of by the
goddesses. 'They flourished on the cheese, the sweet
honey and the mellow wine that Aphrodite brought
them, while Hera made them beautiful and wise
beyond all other women, chaste Artemis increased
their stature, and Athena taught them the skilled
handicrafts that are a woman's pride. But there
came a day when Aphrodite, eager to make happy
marriages for them all, went up to high Olympus to
consult with Zeus . . . and on that very day the
Harpies snatched them up and gave them to the
hateful Erinyes to serve their beck and call' (E.V.
Rieu, 1946).

   In the drawing Pandareus can be seen in the foreground hiding from Zeus' anger. The voluptuous
poses of the daughters and the portrayal of the
goddesses, Artemis, Aphrodite, Hera and Athena
in the vein of Offenbach's operettas are examples of
Fuseli's gradual transition to an ironic, parodistic
approach to Greek mythology.

66 Achilles Grasps at the Shade of Patroclus
   [c.1810]
   (Homer, *Iliad*, XXIII, 99–101)

Pencil, watercolour, heightened with white
chalk, 35 × 59.6 cm
Exh: Zurich 1926 (290); 1941 (175); 1969
(232); London 1950 (122); New York 1954
(15); Bremen/Dusseldorf 1957 (122)
Lit: Federmann 1927, p.64, pl.51 top;
Ganz 1947, 73
Schiff: 1358
Zurich, Kunsthaus, Inv. No.1916/22

For the subject see No.59

**67 Achilles Sacrifices his Hair on the Funeral
Pyre of Patroclus** [1800–1805]
(Homer, *Iliad*, XXIII, 141)

Ink and watercolour, 48.0 × 31.5 cm
Inscr. at bottom from the *Iliad*: Ξανθην
απεκειρατο χαιτην
('. . . he cut off from his head an auburn
lock. . .')
Exh: Zurich 1926 (256); 1941 (164); 1969
(233); London 1950 (100); Bremen/Dussel-
dorf 1957 (123)
Lit: Federmann 1927, p.65, pl.47; Schrade
1931, p.14, note 28; Beutler 1939, p.19 with
repr; Ganz 1947, 71; Antal 1956, pp.99, 218,
note 14, pl.38a; Irwin 1966, p.48, repr. 35
Schiff: 1359
Zurich, Kunsthaus, Inv. No.1916/20

67

Achilles and his men built a pyre for Patroclus. His
body was carried in procession with Achilles as the
chief mourner. When they had laid him on the pyre,
Achilles stepped back and cut off a lock of his own
hair to lay on the body.

68   **With Eëriboea's Help Hermes Rescues Ares**
from the Aloeids 1819–22
(Homer, *Iliad*, V, 383ff.)
Pen and wash, 31.7 × 40.4 cm
Inscr. at bottom edge: 'Petersham Sept.ʳ – 19
Putney Hill May – 22'
Watermark: 'Golding & Snelgrove 1818'
On the back, pencil sketches of the two giants
Schiff: 1515
Munich, Dr Alfred Winterstein (formerly
Richard von Kühlmann, via Karl & Faber,
Munich)

The giants Otus and Ephialtes, the children of
Aloeus, were notorious evil-doers. Once they even
piled Mount Pelion on Mount Ossa in their amorous
pursuit of Hera. In the myth illustrated here they
kept Ares, the god of war himself, imprisoned in a
bronze jar without food for thirteen months. But
their mother, Eëriboea, revealed the hiding place
and sent them to sleep so that Hermes could
release Ares.

69   **Nestor Prevents the Achaeans from Fleeing by**
Telling Them that Thetis and her Nymphs
have Come out of the Sea to Mourn the Dead
Achilles 1813
(Homer, *Odyssey*, XXIV, 47ff.)
Pencil with grey wash, 17.8 × 21.6 cm
Inscr. bottom left in ink: 'Q.E. [Queen's Elm]
Jun. 8. 13'; bottom right, quotation in Greek
from the Odyssey (XXIV, 54): μη φευγετε
κουροι 'Αχαιων
(do not flee Achaean warriors)
Schiff: 1520
Birmingham, City Museum and Art Gallery,
Inv. No.P. 31 60

The soul of Agamemnon recounts to Achilles' soul
the events after the latter's death at Troy:
   And thy mother came forth from the sea with the
   immortal sea-nymphs, when she heard the tidings,
   and a wondrous cry arose over the deep, and
   thereat trembling laid hold of all the Achaeans.
   Then would they all have sprung up and rushed
   to the hollow ships, had not a man wise in the
   wisdom of old, stayed them, even Nestor, whose
   counsel had before appeared the best.
   He with good intent addressed their assembly
   '. . . 'Tis his [Achilles] mother who comes here
   forth from the sea with the immortal sea-nymphs
   to look upon the face of her dead son'. So he
   spoke, and the great-hearted Achaeans ceased
   from their flight (A. T. Murray).

70   **Achilles, Athene's Tasselled Aegis Round his**
Shoulders and a Golden Mist Round his Head,
Takes his Stand by the Trench and Raises the
Warcry (1815)
(Homer, *Iliad*, XVIII, 202ff.)
Pencil with grey wash, 59.7 × 46.6 cm
Watermark: 'John Hall 1814'

On the back, collection stamp of the Countess
of Guilford
Exh: Zurich 1969 (273)
Schiff: 1516
Zurich, Kunsthaus, Inv. No.1940/154

Patroclus has been killed by Hector and Achilles
has at last resolved to avenge his death. The drawing shows Achilles preparing for the fight with the
Trojans:

> When she had thus spoken swift-footed Iris
> departed; but Achilles, dear to Zeus, roused him,
> and round about his mighty shoulders Athene
> flung her tasselled aegis, and around his head the
> fair goddess set thick a golden cloud, and forth
> from the man made blaze a gleaming fire . . .
> Then strode he from the wall to the trench, and
> there took his stand, yet joined him not to the
> company of the Achaeans, for he had regard to
> his mother's wise behest. There stood he and
> shouted, and from afar Pallas Athene uttered
> her voice. . . (A. T. Murray).

**71   Enyo, the Goddess of War, and the Personifi-
cation of Fear Wakes a Sleeping Warrior**
[1790–95]
(free illustration of Aeschylus' *Seven against
Thebes*)
Black chalk with ink and wash, 67.0 × 53.5 cm
Inscr. bottom right: Ἀρην Ἐνυω και
φιλαιματον φοβον
(Ares, Enyo and bloodthirsty Fear – Aeschy-
lus, *Seven against Thebes*, v, 45); beside it, '86'
On the back a pencil sketch of a seated man
Exh: Zurich 1969 (186)
Lit: Ganz 1947, 45
Schiff: 985
Zurich, Kunsthaus, Inv. No.1940/140
(formerly Paul Hürlimann)

The drawing evidently illustrates a passage in the
speech of the messenger who informs Eteocles that
the Seven are preparing for war against him and
Thebes, and that they have sworn with Ares, Enyo
(a personification of war, hence sometimes referred
to as Ares' mother, at other times as her daughter)
and bloodthirsty 'Defeat' (or Fear) to destroy the
city and drown the land in blood.

72   Orestes' Vision [*c*.1800]
(Euripides, *Iphigenia in Tauris*, 285–91)
Pencil, ink and wash, 43.2 × 57.5 cm
Schiff: 1425
*London, Trustees of Sir Colin and Lady
Anderson*

Fuseli chose to illustrate the moment in the play
when Orestes sees three Furies following him. The
first is not described any more fully, the second
frightens him with the snakes she wears in her hair
or slung over her arm. The third one he sees flying
towards him bearing the bloody corpse of his mother

74

in her arms. When she tries to hurl the corpse down on top of him, it suddenly turns into a rock and threatens to crush him to death. Fuseli clearly conceded the impossibility of depicting Clytaemnestra's transformation into the rock and cut the drawing at the level of the Furies' wrists. In another version (Schiff 1420) he includes the piece of rock. Pylades supports Orestes who stumbles back in shock. The Furies are conceived as a formal unit rather like 'threefold' *Hecate* in Blake's monotype of 1795.

73 Hephaestus, Bia and Cratus Chain Prometheus to a Rock in the Caucasian Mountains [1800–10]

(Aeschylus, *Prometheus Bound*, 64–5)

Pencil and watercolour, the contours traced over in ink by a different hand, 35.9 × 30.2 cm
On the reverse sketches of a reclining woman and a man approaching
Lit: Tomory 1967, 24
Schiff: 1790
Auckland, New Zealand, City of Auckland Art Gallery, Inv. No.1965-80

Prometheus is being punished for stealing fire from the Gods and giving it to man.

Cratus commands Hephaestus, the God of Fire: to 'firmly fasten the cruel point of the steel spike through his breast'.

74 The Erinyes Beside Eriphyle's Corpse 1810

Black chalk and ink with grey wash, 20 × 24.3 cm
Inscr. bottom left: 'Q.E. (Queen's Elm) Aug.ᵗ 10.'; on the top edge, in Greek, Clytaemnestra's words from Aeschylus' *Choephoroe*: 924: φυλαξαι μητρος εγκοτους κυνας
(. . . beware the wrathful sleuth-hounds that avenge a mother') (H.W. Smyth)
Schiff: 1807
Zurich, Kurt Meissner (formerly Jürg Stuker, Berne)

Preparatory study for painting No.61, without the figure of Alcmaeon.

Eriphyle was the wife of Amphiaros, one of the Seven Against Thebes. She was killed by her son, Alcmaeon, and instructs the furies (the Erinyes), to pursue her son to avenge her death. This story is similar to that of Clytaemnestra, hence the quotation.

75 The Death of Gaius Gracchus [*c.*1776]
(Plutarch, *G. Gracchus*, 17)
Pen and ink and red wash, 36.2 × 47.0 cm
Lit: Powell 1951, no.21; Antal 1956, p.42;
Irwin 1966, p.47, repr. 34
Schiff: 403
London, Trustees of the British Museum,
Roman Album, fol.24r, No.28, Inv.
No.1885-3-14-226

Like two other similar drawings (Schiff 401, 402)
this was possibly a preparatory study for the lost
painting of 'Gaius Gracchus Dying near the Temple
of the Fates, Invoking them to Revenge his Cause
on Rome' which was exhibited in the Society of
Artists in 1778. The word 'Fates' is a mistake; in
Plutarch the reference is to the 'Furies'. The motif
of calling on the furies is Fuseli's own elaboration
of the Plutarch text which merely states that the
death of Gracchus took place at the sanctuary of the
furies.

A riot broke out in Rome in the 2nd century BC
partly over Gracchus' proposed revolutionary re-
forms. The opposing factions were lead by Opimius
for the Senate and Fulvius Flaccus. Gracchus fled
and was pursued by his foes. He escaped to a sacred
grove (of the Furies) while two friends held back the
pursuers. There he was killed by his servant, Philo-
crates, who then slew himself.

76 Perseus and the Graeae 1771
(Ovid, *Metamorphoses*, IV, 770ff.)
Pen and ink, 43.0 × 50.0 cm
Inscr. bottom: 'Roma May 71'; την χρηυς
χειρεσσι καταπρηγνεσσι λαβουσα
(Homer, *Odyssey*, XIX, 467)
Schiff: 405a
Hamburg, Kunsthalle (formerly R.A. Harari,
Esq., O.B.E.)

In order to obtain the head of the Medusa, Perseus
needed a leather bag, a mirror and a pair of winged
shoes. These were in the possession of some nymphs
whose dwelling-place was known only to the Graeae,
the two daughters of Phorcys. This drawing shows
how Perseus managed to steal the single eye shared
by the two sisters and thus forced them to disclose
the secret. The one he assails does not have it in her
possession at the time, and turns towards her sleeping sister to get hold of the eye so she can see him.
She has just put out her hand to receive it. Athena
points to the sleeping sister, while Perseus looks
over expectantly, his right hand ready to catch hold
of the eye.

The context for the quotation from the Odyssey
'grasping it with her hand, the old woman . . .' is
unconnected with the subject matter of this drawing. The allusion is simply to the outstretched hand.

**77 Galinthias Deceives Eileithyia by Announcing
the Birth of Heracles** [*c.*1772]
(Ovid, *Metamorphoses*, IX, 279ff.; Antoninus
Liberalis, *Metamorphoses*, 29)
Pen and ink and wash, 36.8 × 49.5 cm
Inscr. bottom right: '3'
Exh: Zurich 1926 (94); 1941 (294); New York
1954 (45); Zurich 1965 (128); 1969 (132)
Lit: Mandach 1946, p.32
Schiff: 406
Zurich, Kunsthaus, Inv. No.1940/188 (on
loan from the Gottfried Keller Foundation;
formerly Countess of Guilford and Paul
Hürlimann)

Alcmene conceived a child by Zeus to whom she
wanted to give birth. Hera, in a fit of jealousy, sent
for Eileithyia the goddess of child birth, charging
her to wait outside Alcmene's house and cast a spell
over her. By crossing her right leg over her left leg
and her hands over her knees, she prolonged Alcmene's labour pains for seven days and nights, thus
preventing the birth from taking place. Seeing that
Alcmene was about to collapse with pain, her servant maid Galinthias hit on a cunning idea. She
sprang out of the bedroom, surprising the goddess,

75

76

77

78

80

83

and announced that Alcmene had just given birth
to a boy. Eileithyia's astonishment and shock at the
failure of her spell caused her to relinquish her
magical grip. At that very moment, Heracles was
born. However Eileithyia punished Galinthias by
transforming her into a weasel, which according to
the ancient myth gives birth through the mouth –
and Galinthias had enabled Alcmene to give birth
'through the mouth', i.e. through her cunning
words.

In the background of Fuseli's drawing we see the
woman in labour, her head thrown back in pain. A
maid-servant is looking to her needs. Galinthias approaches the goddess and touches her knee, as if to
emphasise the breaking of the spell by touch. In
accordance with the theory of the fruitful moment
that includes past, present and future, the goddess
is already loosening the grip on her legs, but still
holds her hands tightly clasped, indicating that her
spell is about to break. At Galinthias' feet Fuseli
includes two weasels as an allusion to the metamorphosis the servant maid would have to undergo.

78 Prometheus [c.1770–71]

Pen and ink and wash over pencil,
15.0 × 22.6 cm
Inscr. on the rock in sepia: 'M.A.B.'
(Michelangelo Buonarotti)
On the back, an ink drawing of a male nude
Exh: Zurich, 1959 (4); 1969 (163)
Lit: Schiff 1959, 4
Schiff: 629
Basle, Öffentliche Kunstsammlung, Inv.
No.1917.186 (formerly Arnold Otto Meyer,
Hamburg)

This composition stems from an artistic exercise
Fuseli drew up with the English sculptor Thomas
Banks at the beginning of his study period in Rome.
The exercise consisted of drawing figures round five
arbitrarily placed dots indicating the position of the
head, hands and feet. The figures naturally acquired
strange postures which brought with them difficult
problems of anatomy and fore-shortening. Fuseli
and Banks often worked on identical sets of dots
and then compared the results (cf. C.F. Bell, *Annals
of Thomas Banks*, Cambridge 1938, p.9). It is typical
of Fuseli that such an intellectual, contrived process
should replace the direct study from nature. In
these experiments he frequently seems to have been
unsatisfied with the nude study itself and, as in the
case of *Prometheus* turned it into a specific theme.

79 Perseus Frees Andromeda 1778

Version of a Roman relief in the Capitoline
Museum, Rome (Stuart Jones, Pl.53, No.89)

Pen and ink and wash, 40.1 × 27.2 cm
Inscr. bottom right: 'Roma Febr. 78';
below: '27'
Exh: Zurich 1926 (117); 1941 (244); Bremen/

79

Dusseldorf 1957 (67)
Lit: Ganz 1947, 25; Hofmann 1952, p.172;
Antal 1956, pp.41, 52, 91, 93
Schiff: 659
Zurich, Kunsthaus, Inv. No.1940/60
(formerly Paul Hürlimann)

Andromeda's mother, Queen of Ethiopia, boasted
that Andromeda was far more beautiful than the
Nereids who complained to Poseidon. In anger
Poseidon flooded the land and sent a monster to
ravage it. To appease Poseidon, Andromeda had to
be sacrificed to the monster and was fastened to a
rock on the seashore. At this point Perseus happened
to pass by. He fell in love with Andromeda and
rescued her from the rock after killing the monster.

80   The Three Fates 1781

Black chalk on oiled paper, 41.5 × 31.0 cm
Inscr. bottom right: 'Decr 81'
Exh: Zurich 1926 (156); 1941 (282); New
York 1954 (37); Zurich 1969 (171)
Schiff: 808
Zurich, Kunsthaus, Inv. No.1938/704
(Ganz Bequest)

Study for the painting *Psyche, unperturbed, passing
the Fates*, based on Apuleius, *Metamorphoses*, VI, 20
(Schiff 715)

81

81   Perseus Returns the Eye to the Graeae
[*c*.1790–1800]
(Apollodorus, II, 4, 2)

Pen and ink and wash, 19.0 × 16.9 cm
Schiff: 987
Birmingham, City Museum and Art Gallery

In contrast to the drawing of 1771 in the Hamburg
Kunsthalle (No.76) in which Perseus is stealing the
eye from the Graeae, Fuseli here depicts all three
sisters. This indicates that he is following Apollodorus rather than Ovid.

82   Heracles Kills the Horses of Diomedes 1798
(Apollodorus, II, 5, 8; Quintus Symrnaeus,
VI, 247–50)

Pen and sepia and wash, 28.5 × 20.0 cm
Inscr. bottom left: '14 May 98'; on the back
of the mount: 'Heinr. Füssli/Herakles und
die Rosse des Diomedes'
Schiff: 989
Zurich, Private collection

Fuseli combines two different versions of the saga.
Heracles is depicted carrying the body of Abderus,
his friend and son of Hermes. According to Apollodorus Abderus was left in charge of the stolen horses
while Heracles was challenged to a fight by the Bistones under Diomedes on the sea shore. But Abderus could not control the horses and they devoured him. Heracles fought with the Bistones,
killed Diomedes, forced the others to flee and

82

founded the city of Abdera on the site of Abderus' tomb. He then brought the mares to Eurystheus. Fuseli, however, both in this drawing and a later version of the theme (Schiff 1371) depicts the fight taking place in a stable with the remains of the prisoners thrown to the horses lying around on the ground, while Heracles is intent on killing king and horses. Hyginus, *Fabulae*, XXX is also ruled out as a possible source for this version since he explicitly states that Heracles slaughtered Diomedes and his four mares with the help of Abderus. So we are left with Quintus of Smyrna's continuation of the *Iliad*, according to which Heracles killed the king and the horses 'beside the wretched crib', no mention being made of Abderus.

83 Pasiphaë, Besotted with Love for the Bull, Searches for Herbs and Plants [c.1805–10]
(Virgil, *Eclogue* VI)

Pencil and chalk and sepia, 12.5 × 20.0 cm
Inscr. on either side: 'Ah virgo infelixa qua te dementia cepit'; 'Ah virgo infelix tu nunc per gramina curris' (Virgil, Eclog. VI, 47, 52, quoted from memory; line 52 concludes with the words 'in montibus erras')
Watermark: '1805'
Exh: Zurich 1941 (378); 1969 (241)
Lit: Mandach 1946, p.32
Schiff: 1375
Zurich, Kunsthaus, Inv. No.1934/4 (on loan from the Gottfried Keller Foundation)

This myth relates how Minos has asked Poseidon to send him a sign to show that he, and not another, should be King of Crete. In answer Poseidon sends a bull for sacrifice but Minos is so overcome by the beast's beauty he does not perform the necessary sacrifice. Poseidon in anger, causes Pasiphaë, Minos' wife, to fall desperately in love with the bull.

Fuseli depicts Pasiphaë in search of herbs to feed the bull, or of aphrodisiac plants for a love potion; see the "magic" circle with her footsteps.

The inscriptions read: 'O unfortunate lady what madness has seized you'; 'O unhappy lady now you run through the grass'.

84 Bacchanalian Scene 1812
(Livy, XXXIX, 8)

Pencil and wash on white paper,
40.6 × 31.9 cm
Inscr. bottom right in pencil: 'Q.E. [Queen's Elm] May 12.'; in a different hand: '90'
On the reverse tracing of the female figure
Exh: Zurich 1926 (292); 1941 (391)
Schiff: 1530
Zurich, Kunsthaus, Inv. No.1940/195 (on loan from the Gottfried Keller Foundation)

An obstinate novice is to be executed and even on the execution block rejects the priestess's offer to save her life if she will take part in the orgy. In the background, dancing bacchantes. Fuseli took his inspiration for this drawing from Livy's account of the discovery of the secret cult of the bacchanals by Consul Spurius Posthumius Albinus (reference by Andreas Rumpf).

85 With an Arrow Heracles Kills Ladon, the Dragon that Guards Hera's Golden Apple Tree, at the Foot of which the Terrified Hesperides Huddle Together 1814
(Apollonius Rhodius, *Argonautica*, 4, 433ff.)

Pencil, 31.8 × 39.9 cm
Inscr. bottom left: 'Apollon. R. △433 etc; bottom right; 'K. [Knavestoke] Aug! 4.14.'
On the back, a profile sketch of a dancing girl in a thin dress, facing right
Exh: Zurich 1926 (345); 1941 (414)
Schiff: 1528
Basle, Öffentliche Kunstsammlung, Inv. No.1914. 132.22.

This illustrates one of the twelve labours of Heracles.

84

85

Milton and the Bible

86 The Shepherd's Dream (1793)
  (Milton, *Paradise Lost*, I, 781ff.)
  Painting No.4 of the 'Milton Gallery'

  Oil on canvas, 154 × 215 cm
  Exh: Zurich 1969 (43)
  Lit: Haydon-Hazlitt 1838, p.214; Schiff 1963,
  p.142, passim; Macandrew 1963, p.210, 212
  Schiff: 1762; cf. No.101
  London, Tate Gallery, Inv. No.T.876

The verses on which this painting is based occur in a significant context in Milton's text. In hell, in the overfilled hall of pandemonium, the lower ranks of the fallen angels shrink to the size of dwarfs in order to make more room; Milton compares them with the fairies who bewitch a countryman who has fallen asleep in a wood with their music and dancing. In English folklore fairies are said to be diminutive. The comparison suggested itself to Milton because of a tradition which held that fairies were originally fallen angels.

Fuseli varies and elaborates the motif. Instead of depicting the fairies on the ground dancing in a magic circle, as they were commonly represented in traditional woodcuts, he has them fluttering about over the head of the sleeping shepherd. One of them touches him with the dream-inducing magic wand. Robin Goodfellow-Puck can be seen hovering in front of the moon. Beneath the left-hand fairy, Ariel is riding on a bat (*The Tempest*, V, 1). In the lower left-hand corner crouches a witch who has just pulled a blossom-headed mandrake out of the ground. Queen Mab, the bringer of nightmares, is seated on the steps in the lower right-hand corner; the monstrous child she holds on a chain is the demonic incubus. The latter is pointing at the sleeping man and is about to move towards him, to press him. The naked fairy combing her hair further up the steps derives from Shropshire folklore.

According to this tradition such apparitions entice the traveller and ask him for one of his garments; they then overpower him, steal all his clothes, and leave him wretchedly scratched and pulled about. The building is either a temple of Diana, for in medieval folklore she was transformed into a demon who led the wild army of witches through the sky at night; or alternatively, it is the ivory portal through which, according to Homer (*Odyssey*, XIX, 526–67) and Virgil (*Aeneid*, VI, 893–6), delusive dreams emerge. Fuseli may also have had in mind various Swiss traditions which revolve round a legendary 'temple of Isis' and still persist today, for instance in the name of a hill at Benken (Canton of Zurich) known as the 'Isenbuck'.

87 Sin, Pursued by Death [1794–6]
(Milton, *Paradise Lost*, II, 787ff.)
Painting No.7 of the 'Milton Gallery'

Oil on canvas, 119 × 132 cm
Exh: Zurich 1936 (34); 1941 (42); Paris 1948 (113); Geneva 1948 (197); London 1950 (17); Bremen/Dusseldorf 1957 (27); Zurich 1969 (37)
Lit: Anon. 1805, p.369; Fuseli 1806, p.399; Leslie 1854, p.136ff.; quoted by Todd 1946 pp. 76-8; Thornbury 1860, p.135; Federmann 1927, p.170; Schiff 1963, pp.51, 55, 144; Hofsttäter 1965, p.193
Schiff: 892; cf. Nos.92, 100
Zurich, Kunsthaus (on loan from the Gottfried Keller Collection)

According to Milton's personal mythology, Sin sprang out of Satan's head as Pallas had done out of the head of Zeus. With Sin, Satan gave birth to death (cf. No.100). When the latter also had possessed Sin, she had to give endless birth to the hounds of hell. The following lines are illustrated:

I fled, and cried out *Death*!
Hell trembled at the hideous name, and sighed
From all her caves, and back resounded *Death*!
I fled, but he pursued (though more, it seems,
Inflamed with lust than rage) and swifter far,
Me overtook, his mother, all dismayed,
And in embraces forcible and foul
Engend'ring with me, of that rape begot

88 Satan Bursts from Chaos [1794–6]
(Milton, *Paradise Lost*, II, 1010ff.)
Painting No.11 of the 'Milton Gallery'

Oil on canvas, 126 × 101 cm
Exh: Zurich 1941 (46); Bremen/Dusseldorf 1957 (25); Zurich 1969 (38)
Lit: Timbs 1860, p.192; Haydon 1960-63, III, p.18; Schiff 1963, passim, repr. 22
Schiff: 893
Zurich, Private collection (formerly Countess of Guilford)

On his flight Satan is shown the way to the newly created world by Chaos, the ruler of the as yet uncreated regions. Chaos can be seen, arm outstretched at the lower left-hand corner seated on his throne in his 'dark pavilion' rendered as a Doric temple (V. 960): beside him Night and Orcus, and Hades with arms flung wide. The illustration is taken from the following lines:

He ceased; and Satan stayed not to reply,
But glad that now his sea should find a shore,
With fresh alacrity and force renewed
Springs upward like a pyramid of fire
Into the wild expanse.

89 Odysseus between Scylla and Charybdis
[1794–6]
(Milton, *Paradise Lost*, II, 1019ff.)
Painting No.12 of the 'Milton Gallery'

Oil on canvas, 126 × 101 cm
Exh: Zurich 1941 (62); Paris 1948 (122); Geneva 1948 (206); Bremen/Dusseldorf 1957 (335); Zurich 1969 (39)
Lit: Schiff 1963, repr. 23, pp.61, 145
Schiff: 894
Aarau, Aargauer Kunsthaus

Milton uses the motif of the Odyssey as an allegory for Satan's safe flight back to earth through the hostile elements after his visit to Chaos saying he is 'harder beset' than

When Ulysses on the larboard shunned
Charybdis and by the other whirlpool steered

In the centre of the composition Odysseus, striking the pose of the 'Borghese Gladiator', raises his shield to protect himself from the Scylla who is depicted as a towering rock from which project three of her six heads, all busily engaged in devouring Odysseus' six companions who have been swept overboard. A further abyss is indicated by a gaping hole in the rock. To the right of the scene the water level drops suddenly, denoting Charybdis' whirlpool.

90 The Creation of Eve (1793)   (colour repr. p.22)
(Milton, *Paradise Lost*, VIII, 426-70)
Painting No.17 of the 'Milton Gallery'

Oil on canvas, 307 × 207 cm
Exh: Bremen/Dusseldorf 1957 (112)
Lit: Young 1823, No.41; Timbs 1860, p.193; Macandrew 1959 (60); p.20ff.; Schiff 1963, passim, repr. 31; Hofstätter 1965, p.193; Irwin 1966, p.133, 137
Schiff: 897
Hamburg, Kunsthalle (formerly John Julius Angerstein; Dr W. von Burg, Lausanne; Carl Laszlo, Basle)

In two letters to William Roscoe, dated 14 August and 15 September 1795, Fuseli defended himself against any possible theological objections to this picture. The figure of the creator in the background is not meant to represent God,' . . . for believers, let it be the Son, the Visible Agent of his father; for others it is merely a superior Being entrusted with (Eve's) creation, and looking up for approbation of this work to the inspiring power above.' In complying with the ban on depicting God in human form Fuseli shows to what extent he continued to be influenced by his Zwinglian training. He knows that in *Paradise Lost* Christ is entrusted with the task of creation; since he himself is no longer a believer in the full sense he prefers to interpret the mysterious figure as an unspecified 'superior being'.

90

The following lines are illustrated:

> Though sleeping, where I lay, and saw the shape
> Still glorious before whom awake I stood;
> Who stooping opened my left side, and took
> From thence a rib, with cordial spirits warm,
> And life-blood streaming fresh; wide was the wound,
> But suddenly with flesh filled up and healed.
> The rib he formed and fashioned with his hands;
> Under his forming hands a creature grew,
> Man-like, but different sex, so lovely fair
> That what seemed fair in all the world seemed now Mean

(Milton, *Paradise Lost*, VIII, 463-73)

91

91 The Vision of the Deluge [1796–1800]
(Milton, *Paradise Lost*, XI, 742ff.)
Second version of Painting No.25 of the 'Milton Gallery'

Oil on canvas, 158 × 119 cm
Exh: London, Royal Academy, 1818 (226); Zurich 1941 (47); 1969 (40)
Lit: Schiff 1963, pp.74, 151, repr. 35
Schiff: 901
Winterthur, Kunstmuseum

Like the 'Vision of the Lazar House' (No.102) this is one of the images with which the Archangel Michael confronts Adam as a result of the Fall.

92

92 Satan and Death Separated by Sin (1802)
(Milton, *Paradise Lost*, II, 702ff.)
Study for the engraving by J. Neagle in Du Roveray's edition of *Paradise Lost*, London 1802

Oil on canvas, 91 × 40.5 cm
Exh: Zurich 1969 (70)
Schiff: 1210; cf.Nos.87, 100
Munich, Bayerische Staatsgemäldesammlungen, Inv. No.9494 (formerly Scheidwimmer and Samuel

93 The Triumphant Messiah (1802)
(Milton, *Paradise Lost*, VI, 824ff.)
Engraved by C. Warren in Du Roveray's edition of *Paradise Lost*, London 1802

93

Oil on canvas, 91 × 71 cm
Exh: Zurich 1941 (45); 1969 (73)
Lit: Timbs 1860, p.193
Schiff: 1213
Zurich, Private collection

The Messiah is shown above in the heavenly war chariot, encircled by light. Satan, holding his shield up protectively behind him, floats downwards. Beneath the black clouds the rebel angels can be seen plunging down head first; the angel on the extreme right is based on the so-called 'miserly' figure among the damned in Michelangelo's *Last Judgement*. The lines illustrated are:

So spake the Son, and into terror changed
His count'nance, too severe to be beheld
And full of wrath bent on his enemies.
At once the Four spread out their starry wings
With dreadful shade contiguous, and the orbs
Of his fierce chariot rolled, as with the sound
Of torrent floods, or of a numerous host.
He on his impious foes right onward drove,
Gloomy as night; under his burning wheels
The steadfast empyrean shook throughout,
All but the throne itself of God.

94   The Expulsion from Paradise (1802)
(Milton, *Paradise Lost*, XII, 645)
Engraved by A. Smith in Du Roveray's edition of *Paradise Lost*, London 1802.

Oil on canvas, 92 × 71 cm
Exh: Zurich 1941 (48); Bremen/Dusseldorf 1957 (30); Zurich 1969 (74)
Lit: Deonna 1943, p.203
Schiff: 1214
Basle, Private collection (formerly Felix Witzinger and Paul Ganz)

An illustration to the following lines:

Some natural tears they dropped, but wiped them soon;
The world was all before them, where to choose
Their place of rest, and Providence their guide:
They hand in hand, with wand'ring steps and slow,
Through Eden took their solitary way.

95   Solitude at Dawn [1794–6]
(Milton, *Lycidas*)

Oil on canvas, 95 × 102 cm
Exh: London, Royal Academy 1871 (38); Zurich 1926 (60), (pl.XXIV); 1941 (86); Bremen/Dusseldorf 1957 (48); Zurich 1969 (41)
Lit: Anon. 1805, p.372; Fuseli 1806, p.399; Federmann 1927, pl.3; Sitwell 1943, p.228; Gradmann/Cetto 1944, p.75, repr. 68; Macandrew 1959/60, p.33; Schiff 1963, pp.86. 156; Macandrew 1963, pp.214, 217, 220; Hofstätter 1965, p.181
Schiff: 904
Zurich, Kunsthaus (formerly Paul Ganz)

95

This is the earliest of three versions of the theme
executed between May 1794 and August 1796. The
motif of the shepherd goes back to 'The Shepherd's
Dream' (Nos.86,101). In this version Fuseli has retained certain elements, such as the hand laid protectively over the head and the dog roused by the
spirits, which are only meaningful in the context of
fairy magic. In the subsequent versions he deleted
them. Milton dedicated *Lycidas* to the memory of
his childhood friend, Edward King, who died by
drowning. The sleeping figure contains several allegorical allusions to the friend as he is mourned and
glorified in the elegy: Fuseli hints at his budding
personality, the poetic vocation towards which he
moves in the Arcadian Spring of youth, and finally
the integration of these unfulfilled hopes in the
higher existence into which he is to be wafted by
his sudden death.

96   Faery Mab (1793)
       (Milton, *L'Allegro*, 102)
       Painting No.30 in the 'Milton Gallery'

       Oil on canvas, 70 × 91 cm
       Exh: Zurich 1926 (20); 1941 (35); Geneva
       1948 (218); Zurich 1969 (46)
       Lit: Jaloux 1942, p.79; Ganz 1947, p.18;
       Macandrew 1959/60, p.46;
       Schiff: 1963, pp.94,153; Macandrew 1963,
       p.210
       Schiff: 909
       Basle, Private collection

96

The painting illustrates the line 'How Faery Mab
the junkets eat'. Junket is the food traditionally put
out by country people at night for the fairies. Behind Mab appears the Brownie, her dwarflike companion.

**97   Euphrosyne or Mirth, with Fancy and
       Moderation Hovering Over Her, Tripping
       Forward** (1799–1800)
       (Milton, *L'Allegro*)
       Painting No.45 of the 'Milton Gallery'

       Oil on canvas, 243 × 153 cm
       Exh: Zurich 1941 (20); Bremen/Dusseldorf
       1957 (23); Zurich 1969 (44)
       Lit: Knowles 1831, I, p.261; Cunningham
       1857, p.XC; Federmann 1927, p.57;
       Macandrew 1959/60, p.48ff.; Schiff 1963, repr.
       46, pp.27, 90ff., 122, 160; Macandrew, 1963,
       p.219ff.
       Schiff: 907
       Heidelberg, Kurpfälzisches Museum

97

Euphrosyne, or Mirth, with the personifications of
fancy and moderation hovering above her, is seen
skipping lightly towards the spectator. She is accompanied by the 'Wanton Wiles', 'Sport that
wrinkled Care derides' and 'Laughter, holding both
his sides', with Falstaff and Doll in the foreground.
Further back we see the meeting of Zephyros and

98

Aurora, a reference to the birth of Euphrosyne. The formality and seriousness of the composition is hardly appropriate to the theme and was probably due to the fact that when Fuseli was working on it he was depressed about the failure of the first exhibition of his 'Milton Gallery'. In compositional terms it clearly derives from Baroque altar-pieces such as Annibale Carracci's 'Madonna of St. Luke' (1592, Louvre).

98 Silence [1799–1801]
Reproduced as a vignette in an oval frame, engraved by J. Burnet in Henry Fuseli, *Lectures on Painting, delivered at the Royal Academy,* London 1801 (second edition 1830)

Oil on canvas, 63.5 × 51.5 cm
Inscr. at top right: ΣΙΓΑ
Exh: Zurich 1936 (18); 1941 (37); Thun, Thuner Kunstsammlungen 1956 (102); Bremen/Dusseldorf 1957 (24); Zurich 1969 (45)
Lit: Jaloux 1942, p.159; Antal 1956, p.94; Schiff 1963, pp.98, 138, repr. 53
Schiff: 908
Berne, Private collection

The figure is a reinterpretation rather than a modification of the personification of sorrow which crouches beside the main figure in Fuseli's painting of 'Melancholy', an illustration of Milton's *Il Penseroso*, No.46 in the 'Milton Gallery' (preserved in the vignette by J. Sharpe, Schiff 1306). The pose is found in various works by Blake, and most conspicuously in his drawing in the margin of p.47 of Young's *Night Thoughts* (1796-7).

99

99 Milton's Vision of his Second Wife
[1799–1800]
(Milton, *Sonnet XXIII*)

Oil on canvas, 95 × 100 cm
Exh: Zurich 1926 (46); 1941 (38); 1969 (51)
Lit: Macandrew 1959/60, p.49; Schiff 1963, pp.108, 139, note 348, repr. 60; Hofstätter 1965, p.158, pl.31; Macandrew 1963, p.219
Schiff: 920
Basle, Private collection

The painting illustrates *Sonnet XXIII*, which Milton wrote after the death of his second wife, Catherine; she died in child-birth a year after their marriage. Milton was by this time completely blind. His wife appears in the pose of the Hellenistic statue known in his time as the 'Borghese Psyche', now identified as Diana.

100 Satan and Death Separated by Sin 1776
(Milton, *Paradise Lost*, II, 702ff.)

Pen and sepia with brown and grey wash, 26.2 × 37.7 cm
Inscr. bottom right: 'Roma oct. 76'
Another drawing partly visible on the right

Lit: Knowles 1831, I, p.205; Federmann 1927,
pl.37b; Ganz 1947, 18; Lankheit 1951, p.175;
Hofmann 1952, p.170; Antal 1956, p.53;
Schiff 1959, 15; Schiff 1963, repr. 13, p.50;
Winner 1965, p.278
Schiff: 480
Oxford, Visitors of the Ashmolean Museum
(formerly Grete Ring, M. and L. Bollag,
John Knowles)

On the left Satan, bewinged and bright; above him
to the right Death, black, with a crown on his head.
Death aims at Satan with the spear he brandishes
in his left hand. Satan, on the other hand, has low-
ered his spear and gazes at Sin rising between them.
She is explaining to him that she has given birth to
Death as the result of his embrace, and that they
must all three work together towards the destruction of the human race.

The lines illustrated are as follows:
    So frowned the mighty combatants that hell
    Grew darker at their frown, so matched they
    stood;
    For never but once more was either like
    To meet so great a foe. And now great deeds
    Had been achieved, whereof all hell had rung,
    Had not the snaky sorceress that sat
    Fast by hell gate, and kept the fatal key,
    Ris'n, and with hideous outcry rushed between.
(cf. Nos.87, 92)

101 The Shepherd's Dream [1786]
(Milton, *Paradise Lost*, I, 781ff.)

Pencil and red chalk with grey wash,
40.0 × 55.2 cm
Inscr. on the passe-partout: 'Vision tirée
du poeme de Spencer [sic] intitulée: The
Fairy-Queen'
Exh: London, Royal Academy, 1786
Lit: Hofmann 1952, p.163ff., with repr.
Antal 1956, p.104, pl.46; Schiff 1961, p.6ff.,
repr 2; Schiff 1963, p.82ff., repr. 42
Schiff: 829
Vienna, Albertina, Inv. No.14652 (from the
collection of Archduke Albert of
Sachsen-Teschen)

This is a study for No.86.

102 The Vision of the Lazar House [1791–3]
(Milton, *Paradise Lost*, XI, 477-490)

Pencil with some wash, heightened with white,
56.5 × 66.0 cm
Exh: Zurich 1926 (246); 1941 (348); London
1950 (91); Bremen/Dusseldorf 1957 (113);
Zurich 1969 (199)
Lit: Federmann 1927, pl.51; Ganz 1947, 86;
Lankheit 1951, p.178; Blunt 1959, p.41,
pl.27b; Irwin 1959, p.436, note 1, p.439,
repr. 19; Schiff 1963, passim, repr. 37; Irwin
1966, pp.133, 137; Tomory 1972, repr.101,
passim.

101

102

Schiff: 1023
Zurich, Kunsthaus, Inv. No.1916/10 (from
the collection of the Countess of Guilford)

In Milton's poem the Lazar house is one of the
images of death that the Archangel Michael shows
Adam. A sick man tries to escape, but is fettered by
an iron ball chained to his right foot. A young woman, having apparently tried in vain to restrain
him, sinks down exhausted by his side. A man has
thrown himself in front of the sick man and tries to
pull him to the ground. The fleeing figure points his
right arm towards the sky and looks up to the spectre of death who hovers over the scene with his
wings spread out like a baldachino. Fuseli saw this
protest against death and suffering as a parallel in
earthly terms to Satan's rebellion – it is not in Milton's text. The drawing is based on a sketch (No.7)
made in Rome *c*.1772.

The lines illustrated are:
   Immediately a place
   Before his eyes appeared, sad, noisome, dark,
   A lazar-house it seemed, wherein were laid
   Numbers of all diseased, all maladies
   Of Ghastly spasm, or racking torture, qualms
   Of heart-sick agony, all feverous kinds,
   Convulsions, epilepsies, fierce catarrhs,
   Intestine stone and ulcer, colic pangs,
   Demoniac frenzy, moping melancholy
   And moon-struck madness, pining atrophy,

Marasmus, and wide-wasting pestilence,
Dropsies and asthmas, and joint-racking rheums.
Dire was the tossing, deep the groans; Despair
Tended the sick, busiest from couch to couch;

103

103 Eve at the Forbidden Tree (1794–6)
(Milton, *Paradise Lost*, IX, 780ff.)
Preparatory study for the lost painting No.19
of the 'Milton Gallery'

Pencil, ink and wash, 51.0 × 34.0 cm
Exh: New York 1954 (64); St. Gallen 1957,
Malende Dichter – Dichtende Maler (Painting
poets – Poetising Painters) (235); Zurich
1969 (198)
Schiff: 1022
Zurich, Kunsthaus, Inv. No.1914/33

The following lines are illustrated:
So saying, her rash hand in evil hour
Forth reaching to the fruit, she plucked, she eat.

104 The Vision of Noah [1796–9]
(Milton, *Paradise Lost*, XI, 861ff.)
Preparatory study for painting No.26 of the
'Milton Gallery'

Black and white chalk, 58.7 × 70.5 cm
Exh: Zurich 1926 (165); 1941 (280); 1969 (200)
Lit: Schiff 1963, p.79, repr. 40, p.80
Schiff: 1027
Zurich, Kunsthaus, Inv. No.1938/772

104

God's covenant with Noah is one of the positive
images which the Archangel Michael shows Adam
as a prefiguration of the salvation of mankind.

105 The Lubber Fiend [1793–1810]
[1793–1810]
(Milton, *L'Allegro*, 101-112)

Unsigned engraving (probably by Moses
Haughton) after painting No.32 of the
'Milton Gallery' (1795), 29.3 × 29.7 cm
Lit: Macandrew 1959/60, pp.20ff., 45; Schiff
1963, passim, repr. 48; Macandrew 1963,
pp.210, 219
Schiff: 911
London, Trustees of the British Museum

The 'lubber fiend', Robin Goodfellow or Puck, his
work done, sleeps stretched out over his flail beside an open fireplace. According to English folklore
he is always naked and always leaves a house in a
rage if clothes are laid out for him. Fuseli used the
same pose in 'Thetis mourning the Body of Achilles'
(No.64).

105

The following lines are illustrated:
Then lies him down the lubber fiend
And stretched out all the chimney's length,
Basks at the fire his hairy strength;

106

106 Dalila Visits Samson in the Prison at Gaza
[1800–1805]
(Milton, *Samson Agonistes*, 710ff.)

Pen and wash over pencil, 25.4 × 20.1 cm
Inscr. bottom left: 'P[urser's] C[ross]'
On the reverse, tracing of the figure of Samson
Exh: Zurich 1941 (364); 1959 (33); 1969 (260);
London 1950 (85)
Lit: Schiff 1959, p.33; Powell 1951, p.359,
repr. 65; Schiff 1964, p.132, repr. 88
Schiff: 1414
Zurich, Kunsthaus, Inv. No.1914/19 (formerly
Countess of Guilford)

The figure of Samson is based on the youth in
Michelangelo's 'Sogno' (engraving by Béatrizet,
Passavant, VI, p.119, No.112).

The drawing illustrates the following lines:
But who is this, what thing of sea or land?
Female of sex it seems,
That so bedecked, ornate, and gay,
Comes this way sailing
Like a stately ship . . .

Some rich Philistian matron she may seem,
And now at nearer view, no other certain
Than Dalila thy wife.

107

**107 David Feigns Madness before King Achish
of Gath** [1762–4]
(1 *Samuel*, 21, 14)

Pen and sepia with grey wash, at top left
some zinc white highlights, 27.7 × 32.0 cm
Inscr. bottom right by an unknown hand:
'et David changea sa contenance et contrefit
le fou entre leurs mains|Et il marquoit les
poteaux des portes & faisait couler la salive
sur sa barbe &c,&c,'; stamp of the Countess
of Guilford
Exh: Zurich 1926 (92); 1941 (216); 1969 (115)
Schiff: 322
Zurich, Kunsthaus, Inv. No.1940/200 (on
loan from the Gottfried Keller collection)

The lines illustrated are:
And he [David] changed his behaviour before
them, and feigned himself mad in their hands,
and scrabbled on the doors of the gate, and let
his spittle fall down upon his beard.
Then said Achish unto his servants, Lo, ye see
the man is mad: wherefore then have you
brought him to me?

108

**108 Samuel Appears to Saul in the Presence of the
Witch of Endor** (1777)
(1 *Samuel*, 28)

Pen and sepia wash, 25 × 26.5 cm
Inscr. bottom right: 'Roma Sept. 77'
Faint sketches on back
Lit: Powell 1951, 34; Antal 1956, pp.51, 59,

note 52; p.64, note 106; p.113, note 77
Schiff: 372
London, Victoria and Albert Museum,
Dyce Collection 777

The figure of Samuel is based on the figure of God in Michelangelo's 'Creation of Eve' in the Sistine Chapel. Saul derives from the so-called 'Baccante Morente' in the relief of the same name (cf. H. Dütschke, *Die antiken Marmorbildwerke in Florenz*, Leipzig 1878, No.516). The witch is modelled on the kneeling woman in the foreground of Pellegrino Tibaldi's 'Sermon of John the Baptist' (Bologna, S. Giacomo Maggiore) which Fuseli knew from Zanotti's book of engravings after the paintings of Tibaldi and Niccolos dell'Abbate (Venice 1756).

Saul has come to the witch of Endor in order to speak to the spirit of Samuel. The Philistines have gathered to fight against Israel and Saul wants advice. Samuel announces that the Philistines will defeat the Israelites and that Saul and his sons will be killed. The lines illustrated are as follows:

> Then Saul fell straightway all along the earth,
> and was sore afraid, because of the words of
> Samuel: and there was no strength in him; . . .

109 Unidentified Scene (Perhaps a free Interpretation of the Conversion of St. Paul)

[1778–80]

(*Acts of the Apostles*, 9, 1–8)

Pen and ink and wash, 37.7 × 26.7 cm
Lit: Mason 1951, p.51, 345ff., repr. 6; Antal 1956, pp.41, 47, 104; Irwin 1966, p.57, repr. 61
Schiff: 491
London, Trustees of the British Museum,
Roman Album, fol.15R, No.18, Inv. No.1885-3-14-216

In a letter dated 20 June 1961 Erwin Panofsky postulated the following interpretation of this drawing:

> The composition is based on Michelangelo's fresco in the Cappella Paolina (the escaping horse) and Caravaggio's painting in S. Maria del Popolo (the arms stretched upwards). The extreme foreshortening of the main figure may reveal the additional influence of Hans Baldung's woodcut Curjel 85 (with his 'Gothick' inclinations Fuseli certainly had some interest in Baldung and may also have thought of another Baldung woodcut, the frightened horses in Curjel 82). That Fuseli conceived of St. Paul as a young Roman warrior is not surprising. The future Apostle is explicitly called 'young' in Acts 7:58, and he was represented as a youthful soldier not only by Caravaggio but also by Raphael (Vatican tapestries), Signorelli, and many other artists (cf. Walter Friedlaender,

109

110

Caravaggio Studies, pp.18–28). The original and rather impressive idea of the drawing is, however, that St. Paul, having been thrown off his horse by the divine apparition, is being deprived of all his worldly and military adjuncts: his spear, his parazonium and even his mantle are being carried off by heavenly spirits. He faces God, not only as a man 'reborn' but as a man 'newly born' – restored to the original state in which he is a pure receptacle of Divine Grace. In certain regions an infant to be baptised has to be nude; see Maupassant's novel *Monsieur Parent*: ' . . . Faut attendre l'bon Dieu tout nu.'

111

110 God Puts a Mark on Cain after he Killed Abel
1781

(*Genesis*, 4, 15)

Black chalk heightened with white, the figure of Cain touched up with ink and black wash, 63 × 53.1 cm
Inscr. below: 'Nov. 81'
On the back a study of a head in pencil
Exh: Zurich 1926 (155); 1941 (277); 1969 (168)
Schiff: 791
Zurich, Kunsthaus, Inv. No.1938/769

Cain's pose derives from the figure of the horse-tamer on the Monte Cavallo in Rome, erroneously attributed to Phidias; the figure of God derives from Michelangelo's fresco 'The Creation of the Planets' in the Sistine Chapel.

The lines illustrated are:
> And the Lord said unto him,
> Therefore whosoever slayeth Cain,
> Vengeance shall be taken on him
> Sevenfold. And the Lord set a
> mark upon Cain, lest any finding
> him should kill him.

111 David Slays Goliath [1780–85]

(1 *Samuel*, 17, 49)

Pen and sepia with grey wash, some contours gone over by another hand, 34.3 × 31.1 cm
Inscr. at bottom in an unknown hand: 'David & Goliath'
Exh: Zurich 1969 (170)
Lit: Tomory 1967, 6
Schiff: 1753
Auckland, New Zealand, City of Auckland Art Gallery, Inv. No.1965-79

The illustrated lines are:
> And David put his hand in his bag,
> and took thence a stone, and slang it,
> and smote the Philistine in his forehead,
> that the stone sunk into his forehead;
> and he fell upon his face to the earth.

Dante

112 The Strangling of Duke Alphons of Aragon
[1805]

Pencil with grey wash, 38.1 × 48.6 cm
Inscr. bottom right: 'P[urser's] C[ross]';
bottom left in sepia 'P.C. Jun. 06. Jun. 05';
On the back: 'octave decima Mensis Augusti
Alphonsus de Arragonia Dux &c qui in sero
diei quindecimi mensis Julii graviter fuit
vulneratus – cum non vellet huiusmodi
vulneribus mori, in lecto suo fuit strangulatus.
Burchard Diar'; collection stamp of the
Countess of Guilford
Exh: Zurich 1926 (272); 1941 (169); 1969
(256); Bremen/Dusseldorf 1957 (134)
Lit: Mandach 1946, pp.33, 42, repr. p.43
Schiff: 1402
Zurich, Kunsthaus, Inv. No.1940/194 (on
loan from the Gottfried Keller Foundation)
(formerly Arnold Otto Meyer, Hamburg)

The abbreviated quotation comes from *Johannis
Burchardi Argentinensis ... Diarium sive rerum
urbanarum commentari* (1483–1506, edited by
L. Thuasne, III, Paris 1885, p.72f.). It relates how

Alphonsus of Aragon was seriously wounded on the fifteenth day of July and not wishing to die from his wounds was strangled in his bed on the eighteenth day of the month of August. Fuseli shows Lucretia Borgia, the wife of the murdered man, and her brother Cesare, who planned the murder, watching the scene.

113 Wolfram Leads Bertram of Navarre into his Wife's Cell 1812

(Marguerite of Navarre, *Heptameron*, 23rd novella)

Chalk with grey and blue wash, 18 × 20.6 cm
Inscr. on left illegible (covered by mount); bottom right: 'Fuseli'; at right edge: 'Q.E. [Queen's Elm] 28. April 12'
Schiff: 1539
Basle, Private collection

Wolfram keeps his wife imprisoned with the skeleton of her lover in a niche behind an iron grating. She is kneeling in front of the crucifix, playing a guitar, with a crazed expression on her face.

114

114 Two Dancers [1814–20]

(Marino, *L'Adone*, XX, 82)

Pencil and black chalk, 32.5 × 20.4 cm
Watermark: Golding & Snelgrove 1814
On the back a woman reading and the bust of a woman
Exh: Zurich 1959 (48); 1969 (277)
Schiff: 1538
Basle, Öffentliche Kunstsammlung,
Inv. No.1914.132.19

There is no documentary evidence for Fuseli deriving subject-matter from G.B. Marino's *L'Adone* (1623). However this drawing possibly illustrates the dances described in Canto XX, 76–86, during the festival held in honour of the dead Adone. Stanza 82 (Faunia and Ardelio, '. . . poscia l'un l'altra in su le braccia alzando/Levarsi in aria e gir senz' ali a volo . . .') fits both the description and the mood of the drawing.

The lines describe how the two figures are leaping and twisting in the air with their arms raised as if in flight.

115

115 Ezzelin and the Repentant Meduna 1817

Pencil, 38.5 × 24.1 cm
Inscr. bottom right: 'M.P. June 17'; on the lining, in the Countess of Guilford's hand: 'Ezzelino – from Mr Knowles'
On the reverse, a sketch of the figure of Oineus in 'Meleager assailed by the Aetolians' (Schiff 1354)
Exh: Zurich 1941 (420)
Lit: Mandach 1947, p.33
Schiff: 1536
Zurich, Kunsthaus, Inv. No.1940/198 (on

loan from the Gottfried Keller Foundation)
(formerly John Knowles, Countess of
Guilford, Paul Hürlimann)

According to a comment made by Fuseli in a letter
to Roscoe on 22 October 1791, he himself invented
the story of the crusader Ezzelin Bracciaferro who,
on returning from the Crusades, murdered his wife
because of her supposed or actual unfaithfulness.
He executed a painted version of the theme in 1779
(Schiff 360). In 1814 this painting aroused the interest of Lord Byron, who looked for the origin of
the motif in Italian literature in vain – until Fuseli
confessed (cf. Byron, *Journal*, 20 March 1814).

116 The Thieves' Punishment 1772
(Dante, *Inferno*, XXIV-XXV)

Pencil and pen and wash, heightened with
white, 46 × 61.2 cm
Inscr. at bottom left in sepia: 'Roma März 72';
beneath that: 'Bolgia de' Serpenti'
Exh: Zurich 1926 (105); 1941 (230); Bremen/
Dusseldorf 1957 (58); Rome 1959 (218);
Zurich 1969 (137)
Lit: Federmann 1927, repr. 33; Antal 1956,
pp.51, 56, note 9; Schiff 1964, p.128, repr.80
Schiff: 424
Zurich, Kunsthaus, Inv. No.1938/766
(Ganz Bequest)

Dante and Virgil observe both the agonies of the
thieves who have been attacked by serpents and the
beginning of a metamorphosis in the course of which
the snakes assume the form of the thieves, who in
turn are transformed into snakes.

117 Dante and Virgil on the Ice of Cocytus 1774
(Dante, *Inferno*, XXXII)   (colour repr. p.23)

Pen and sepia wash with greenish-yellow and
brown-violet watercolour, 39 × 27.4 cm
Inscr. bottom right: 'Roma Aug. 74'; the
Countess of Guilford's collection stamp on
the lining
Exh: Zurich 1926 (109); 1941 (236); New York
1954 (26); Bremen/Dusseldorf 1957 (59);
Zurich 1969 (138)
Lit: Federmann 1927, p.40, pl.31; Schrade
1931, p.14, note 28; Schrade 1931-2, p.139;
Ganz 1947, 17; Hofmann 1947, p.170;
Antal 1952, pp.30, 62, note 86
Schiff: 425
Zurich, Kunsthaus, Inv. No.1916/13

Dante strides over the ice, holding his hands up
towards the heads of Ugolino and Ruggiero. Because Ruggiero had ordered Ugolino and his sons to
be starved to death, Ugolino gnaws at Ruggiero's
skull in eternity. Ugolino raises his head to inform

117

Dante of his fate. Further back on the right the figure of Virgil can be seen beside the heads of the sons of Count Alberti di Magona (lines 41-3). The heads of other frozen traitors can be seen on either side. On a steep rock in the background the feet of two giants are visible.

The motif of the giants' feet cut off by the picture edge is also found in Botticelli's illustrations to the *Inferno*, XXXII (F. Lippmann, *Die Zeichnungen des Sandro Botticelli zur Göttlichen Komödie*, Jahrbuch der preussischen Kunstsammlungen, 4, Berlin 1883, p.63). Various other factors indicate that Fuseli knew the Botticelli illustrations. However the provenance of the Botticelli Codex is unfortunately shrouded in total darkness from the time of its inception right up to its sudden re-emergence in 1803; it is therefore not possible to ascertain whether Fuseli in fact drew on Botticelli's design.

118 Ugolino and his Sons Starving to Death in the Tower [1774–8]
(Dante, *Inferno*, XXXIII)

Pen and sepia on pale beige paper lined with thin cardboard, in a mount, 25.8 × 18.5 cm
Inscr. bottom right in an unknown hand: 'J.F.'; on the cardboard, also by an unknown hand 'Fuseli'
Exh: Zurich 1969 (139)
Schiff: 427; cf. No.121
Zurich, Private collection

118

Ugolino tells Dante how he and his sons were locked in the tower and starved and how he watched his three sons die.

> There he died; and even as thou seest me, saw
> I the three fall one by one, between the fifth
> day and the sixth: whence I betook me,
> already blind, to groping over each, and for (two)
> days called them, after they were dead

(Carlyle 1904)

119 Figure Studies, Including a Sketch for an Illustration to Dante [1770–8]

Bottom row from left to right: A head propped in a hand. The half-length figure of an old man with a head similar to the so-called 'Hellenistic Homer'. Seated figure seen from behind and making a sweeping gesture, possibly a rower.
On the back: Sketch for the figure of Meleager in Schiff 380; traces of the drawing on the front.

Pen over preliminary pencil sketch,
27.3 × 35.1 cm
At the edge some numbers, an arithmetical calculation; on the lining a note of the Dante quotation by L. Binyon
Lit: Powell 1951, p.22; Josephson 1956, I, p.244, repr. 342 (detail)
Schiff: 428
London, Trustees of the British Museum,
Roman Album, fol. 40v, No.55/56,
Inv. No.1885-3-14-248

119

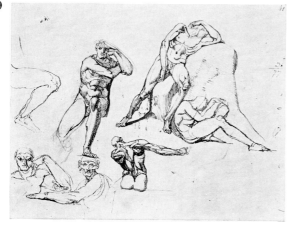

Top row from left to right: A leg. A seated man. Illustration to Dante, *Purgatorio*, IV, 104–8: a rock with a projecting base on which a man lies asleep: one of the weary; to the right of his feet Belacqua ('. . . one|Who seemed to be much wearied, sat him down|And with his arms did fold his knees about|Holding his face between them downward bent.'| H.F. Carey)

Dante characterises Belacqua as a likeable man whose only vice was idleness. He died without doing any penance for his few sins.

120

120 Head of One of the Damned from Dante's Inferno [*c.*1790–92]

> Line engraving, 'dot and lozenge' technique, by William Blake, 35.0 × 26.5 cm
> Exh: London, British Museum, *William Blake and His Circle*, 1957-8, No.22 (5)
> Lit: Keynes 1956, p.76, repr. 42
> Schiff: 946
> *London, Trustees of the British Museum*

Described by Keynes as the head of Satan, this in fact corresponds to the first of the 'Four Heads from Dante's Inferno' in Fuseli's illustrations to Lavaters *Essays on Physiognomy*, II, London 1792, p.290 (*Essai sur la Physiognomie*, II, La Haye 1783, p.260).

121

121 Ugolino and his Sons Starving to Death in the Tower (1806)

> (Dante, *Inferno*, XXXIII)

> Pencil, pen and grey wash, 60.4 × 49.4 cm
> Schiff: 1799a; cf. No.118
> *Chicago, Art Institute*, Leonora Hall Gurley Foundation Collection

Study for the painting of this theme executed in 1806 (Schiff 1200).

122 Dante and Virgil Mounting Geryon 1811

> (Dante, *Inferno*, XVII, 78ff.)

> Pen and ink, 19.8 × 29.3 cm
> Inscr. bottom left: 'Q.E. [Queen's Elm] 8. July. 11'
> On the back, complete tracing of the drawing, with wash
> Exh: Zurich 1969 (276)
> Lit: Tomory 1967, 30
> Schiff: 1808
> *Auckland, New Zealand, city of Auckland Art Gallery*, Inv. No.1965-53

Dante, after visiting the sinners who are being punished in the burning sand, returns to Virgil and the monster Geryon. The drawing illustrates the following lines:

> I found my Guide who had already mounted on the haunch of the dreadful animal; and he said to me: 'Now be stout and bold!'

122

123

123 Dante Swoons Before the Soaring Souls of Paolo and Francesca, Virgil by his Side 1815
(Dante, *Inferno*, V, 80-84)

Black chalk, 32.2 × 20.5 cm
Inscr. at bottom: 'K. [Knavestoke] Jun. 15'
Exh: Zurich 1926 (304); 1941 (407); Bremen/
Dusseldorf 1957 (144)
Lit: Federmann 1927, pl.57; Grigson 1950, p.63
Schiff: 1537
Basle, Öffentliche Kunstsammlung,
Inv. No. 1914. 132.21

Preparatory study for the aquatint engraving (Schiff 1509).

The drawing illustrates:
 Soon as the wind bends them to us,
 I raise(d) my voice: 'O wearied souls!
 Come to speak with us, if none denies it.'
 As doves I called by desire, with (raised) and
 Steady wings (come) through the air to
 Their loved nest, borne by their will:

Northern Poets and Legends

**124 Percival Delivering Belisane from the
Enchantment of Urma** (1783)

    Oil on canvas, 99 × 125 cm   (colour repr. p.24)
    Exh: London, Royal Academy, 1783;
    Zurich 1969 (7)
    Lit: Wilenski 1946, p.51; Tomory 1972,
    pl.III, pp.94ff., 110, 166
    Schiff: 718
    London, Tate Gallery, Inv. No.5304

In a letter to William Roscoe dated 22 October 1791
Fuseli admitted that he had invented the saga of
Percival and Belisane. However in the catalogue of
the Royal Academy exhibition in 1783 he quoted
Kyot, the fictional Provençal inspiration for
Wolfram von Eschenbach's *Parzival*, as his source. In
this painting and its companion piece (Schiff 717)
Fuseli apparently combined motifs from the Klinschor episode from *Parzival* and the third book of
Spenser's *Faerie Queene*. Like Klinschor and Spenser's Busirane, Urma is a magician who separates
women and knights from those they love and holds
them in bondage by means of a spell. As Percival is
about to strike Urma dead, Belisane falls into his
arms, apparently aware that the spell cannot be
lifted without the magician's help. As in *Parzival*
and the *Faerie Queene* the spell is a symbol for the
enslavement of the soul by bodily desires, and Belisane's liberation by her knight symbolizes her purification and preparation for a higher spiritual form
of love.

125

125 Thor Battering the Midgard Serpent [1790]

    Oil on canvas, 131 × 91 cm   (colour repr. p.25)
    Exh: London, British Institution, 1844 (150);
    Manchester, *Art Treasures Exhibition*, 1857
    (104); Leeds 1868 (1284); Philadelphia,
    International Exhibition, 1876; London,
    Roland, Browse & Delbanco, 1948; London,
    Royal Academy, 1951/2 (56); Bournemouth
    1957; Zurich 1969 (6)
    Lit: Cunningham 1830, p.305; Thornbury
    1860, p.135; Federmann 1927, p.175; Irwin
    1966, p.100, repr. 119; Tomory 1972, pl.V,
    p.102ff, 110
    Schiff: 716
    London, Royal Academy of Arts, Diploma
    Gallery

Fuseli's diploma painting which he donated to the
Academy when he was elected a Member in 1790.
He took his theme, deriving originally from the
Edda of Soemundus, from Mallet's *Northern Anti-
quities II* (London 1770, p.134ff.); *The Twenty-
Seventh Fable, of the Journey Undertaken by Thor, to
go to Fish for the Great Serpent*. The figure at the

126

stern of the boat is the giant Hymir, depicted with the same irony as the likeness of Wotan watching from the clouds.

The lines illustrated are:

But Thor assured him that they had better go a good way further: accordingly they continued to row on, till at length Hymir (the giant) told him if they did not stop, they would be in danger from the great Serpent of Midgard. Notwithstanding this, Thor persisted in rowing further, and spite of the Giant, was a great while before he would lay down his oars. Then taking out a fishing line extremely strong, he fixed to it the ox's head, unwound it, and cast it into the sea. The bait reached the bottom, the Serpent greedily devoured the head, and the hook stuck fast in his palate. Immediately the pain made him move with such violence that Thor was obliged to hold fast with both his hands by the pegs which bear against the oars: but the strong effort he was obliged to make with his whole body caused his feet to force their way through the boat and they went down to the bottom of the sea; whilst with his hands, he violently drew up the Serpent to the side of the vessel.

127

126 The Nymphs of the Danube warn Hagen of the Unhappy Outcome of Gunther's Expedition to Kriemhild and Etzel [1800–1815]
(*Nibelungenlied*, XXV, 1577–91)

Oil on canvas, 118 × 142 cm
Exh: Zurich 1926 (55); 1941 (80); London 1950 (27); Bremen/Dusseldorf 1957 (43); Zurich 1969 (65)
Lit: Harcourt-Smith, p.77
Schiff: 1199; cf. No.146
Zurich, Private collection

The nymphs of the Danube warn Hagen that only Gunther's chaplain will survive the journey to Kriemhild and Etzel.

129

127 Kriemhild Throws Herself over the Dead Siegfried [1817–20]
(*Nibelungenlied*, XVII, 1029)

Oil on canvas, 71.5 × 92 cm
Inscr. on the stretcher: 'Crimhild throwing herself over Siffrid's body from das Lied der Niebelungen S.N. [Susan North]'
Exh: Zurich 1941 (77); 1969 (99)
Schiff: 1492
Zurich, Private collection

Hagen brings the dead Siegfried back to Kriemhild. When she discovers his body outside her chamber, she recalls her dream and flings herself upon him.

128 Belinda's Awakening [1780—90]
(Alexander Pope, *The Rape of the Lock*, I)

Oil on canvas, 103 × 126 cm
Lit: Kalman 1971; Tomory 1972, colour
pl.VIII, pp.106, 112ff., 118
Schiff: 1751
*Vancouver, British Columbia, the Vancouver
Art Gallery*

The sleeping Belinda is accompanied by Ariel, who
is about to leave her after finishing his story and
points to the sylph who places the dressing table
with the billet doux in front of her, ready with his
flock to help her with her toilette (145ff.). Shock
kneels at the foot of the bed wrapped in a sheet. He
is about to leap up and wake his mistress (115ff.).
The scene is completed by the demons and incubi
familiar from other works by Fuseli. On Shock's
wrap we see two mating butterflies. The butterfly is
a dream symbol for Fuseli because in Swiss German
dialect the same word 'toggeli' is used for both incubus and butterfly. Beside Ariel's right leg sit the
embodiments of the contrary aspects of Queen Mab
as the sender of both the good and evil dreams. In
the latter guise she is not only endowed with noble
features and elegant attire; she is also distinguished
by a crescent moon, indicating she is a popular
transformation of Diana one of whose attributes

this is. The mischievous figures of Mab to her left as
well as Puck hovering over her have been taken
over from the earlier painting, Cobweb (No.24).
The co-existence of good and bad dreams is familiar
from 'Titania's Awakening' (No.25) and is an inherent feature of Fuseli's imaginary world.

**129 Mathew Complains to Bobadill that he Does
Not Even Have Two Shillings Any More** (1791)
(Ben Johnson, *Every Man in His Humour*;
I, V, in the folio edition of 1616; I, III in the
quarto edition of 1605)
Engraved by Grignion in Vol.IV of *Bell's
British Theatre*, London 1791

Oil on canvas, 60.5 × 51 cm
Exh: Zurich 1926 (31); 1941 (18); Bremen/
Dusseldorf 1957 (13); Zurich 1969 (34)
Lit: Federmann 1927, pl.22; Sitwell 1943,
p.228ff.; Antal 1956, repr. 54a
Schiff: 886
Zurich, Private collection

Master Mathew has come to visit Captain Bobadill
in his lodgings. They decide to go out to a neigh-
bouring tavern. Bobadill who is only just rising
after a late night, gets himself ready and asks
Mathew if he has any money.

130

130 The Fire King Appears to Count Albert
[1801–10]
(Walter Scott, *The Fire King*, a ballad
published in M.G. Lewis, *Tales of Wonder*,
London 1801)

Oil on canvas, 99 × 124 cm
Exh: Zurich 1969 (94)
Lit: Muther 1903, p.92; Tomory 1972, pl.IX,
p.118
Schiff: 1237
London, Victoria and Albert Museum

In Scott's first published work Count Albert, an imprisoned crusader, has given up his Christian faith.
Out of love for the daughter of the Sultan he joins
the army of the infidels. He descends to the cave of
the demon to receive a magic sword.

131 The Poet's Vision [1806–7]
Engraved by A. Raimbach for the frontis-
piece of *Poems by William Cowper, of the Inner
Temple, Esq.*, London (J. Johnson) 1806

Oil on canvas, 61 × 45.5 cm
Exh: Zurich 1926 (37); 1941 (51); Geneva
1948 (217); Zurich 1969 (88)
Schiff: 1229
Basle, Private collection

The poet has fallen asleep on a sofa, lyre in hand.
Over his head appears the poetic muse ready to
crown him with a laurel wreath. Beside her, the
personification of phantasy gazes smilingly at the
sleeping figure. The engraving bears the title 'The
Poet's Vision' and the words 'Sing the Sofa'. 'I
sing the sofa' are the opening words of Cowper's
poem *The Task*. Fuseli's illustration clearly refers
to the muse calling the poet to work.

132 Virtue Calling Youth from the Arms of Vice
[1806–7]   (colour repr. p.26)
(Cowper, *The Progress of Error*, 71–72)
Engraved by W. Bromley in *Poems by William
Cowper, of the Inner Temple, Esq.*, London
(J. Johnson), 1806

Oil on canvas, 91 × 71 cm
Exh: Zurich 1926 (42); 1941 (57); 1969 (89)
Lit: Antal 1956, p.123
Schiff: 1230
Zurich, Private collection

In contrast to the representations of 'Hercules at
the Crossroads' on which this allegory is based,
Fuseli's youth lies oblivious in the arms of vice and
responds to virtue's call with a defiant gesture of self-
vindication. This 'immoral' reinterpretation of the

theme is not without a certain irony; for the youth anticipates the features of the man who was to make his mark on Europe within the next decade as the 'genial immoralist': Lord Byron.

The lines illustrated are:
Is this the rugged path, the steep ascent
That virtue points to? Can a life thus spent
Lead to the bliss she promises the wise,
Detach the soul from earth, and speed her to
the skies?

133 The Negro Revenged [1806–7]
(Cowper, *The Negro's Complaint*, 33–4)
Study for the engraving by A. Raimbach in
*Poems by William Cowper, of the Inner Temple,
Esq.*, London (J. Johnson), 1806

Oil on canvas, 91 × 71 cm
Exh: Zurich 1926 (43); 1941 (58); Paris 1948
(118); Geneva 1948 (202); Bremen/Dusseldorf
1957 (39); Zurich 1969 (91)
Lit: Federmann 1927, p.64; Antal 1956,
pp.124, 130, note 35
Schiff: 1233
Zurich, Private collection
(formerly Paul Ganz)

131

The African and his female companion are watching the sinking of a slave-ship in a tornado, which is interpreted as the punishment meted out by the heavens to the evil slave trade.

The lines illustrated are:
Hark! he answers – Wild tornadoes,
Strewing yonder sea with wrecks;

134 Mad Kate [1806–7]
(Cowper, *The Task*, I, 465)   (colour repr. p.27)
Engraved by W. Bromley in *Poems by William
Cowper, of the Inner Temple, Esq.*, London
(J. Johnson) 1806

Oil on canvas, 91 × 71 cm
Lit: Federmann 1927, pl.20; Todd 1946, pl.29;
Woodward 1950, p.112; Antal 1956, p.122;
Schiff 1963, p.135, note 278; Tomory 1972,
repr. 190
Schiff: 1234
Frankfurt am Main, Goethe-Museum
(formerly Paul Ganz)

132

A serving maid loses her lover at sea and goes mad with grief.

135 The Prison [1806–7]
(Cowper, *The Task*, V, 776–8)
Engraved by C. Warren in *Poems by William
Cowper, of the Inner Temple, Esq.*, London
(J. Johnson), 1806

Oil on canvas, 91 × 71 cm
Exh: Zurich 1926 (41); 1969 (93)
Schiff: 1236
Lausanne, Ambassador Dr Anton Roy Ganz

133

134

135

In Book Five of *The Task* (1785), which is largely political in content, William Cowper wrote that all English spirits would be raised if the walls of the Bastille were to fall; and this, it should be remembered, was five years before the storming of the Bastille. The lines Fuseli chose to illustrate come later in the book, where Cowper discusses the inner freedom of the believer. The theme of the prisoner is mentioned at this point in far more general terms. The scene depicts the personification of this inner freedom appearing in the prison cell to the female companion of the sleeping prisoner. The armed warder waiting at the massive iron grating in the background is an allusion to Raphael's 'The Freeing of St. Peter' in the *Stanza di Eliodoro*.

136 Huon Meets Scherasmin in the Libanon Cave
[1804–5]
(Wieland, *Oberon*, I, 18–19)
Engraved by J. Heath in *Oberon, A Poem from the German of Wieland*, by William Sotheby, Esq. (2nd edition) London 1805

Oil on canvas, 61.3 × 45 cm
Exh: Zurich 1926 (26); 1934 (49); 1941 (22); 1969 (77)
Lit: Federmann 1927, pl.15; Beutler 1939, p.20, repr. Jaloux 1939, p.148
Schiff: 1219
Winterthur, Peter Reinhart (formerly Benjamin Sharpe, Hanwell Park, Middlesex)

The following verses are illustrated:
Sudden the way that led deep rocks among
Sunk in a cavern, from whose pit profound
Sparkled a crackling flame: the stones around,
That o'er the night a wondrous radiance flung,
Were fring'd with bushes, whose rude tangles green
Dangled the mazes of the defts between:
And as they glitter'd with reflected rays,
Shone like a verdant fire. In mute amaze
Motionless stood the knight amid th' enchanted scene.

At once a voice, that thro' the cavern rung,
'Halt!' thunders forth; straight stands the knight before
One of wild mien, whose mantle, cover'd o'er
With cat-skins coarsely patch'd, loose flapping hung
Down to his hairy shanks: in tangled flow,
His coal-black beard thick waved his breast below.
A ponderous branch from giant cedar torn,
Swung, like a mace, upon his shoulder born
Of pow'r the stoutest beast to level at a blow.

137 Scherasmin and Huon Flee from Oberon
[1804–5]
(Wieland, *Oberon*, II, 29–30)
Engraved by F. Engleheart in *Oberon, A*

Poem from the German of Wieland, by William
Sotheby, Esq. (2nd Edition) London 1805

Oil on canvas, 61 × 45 cm
Exh: Zurich 1926 (29); 1941 (23); Bremen/
Dusseldorf 1957 (17); Zurich 1969 (78)
Lit: Federmann 1927, p.16; Jaloux 1942,
p.147
Schiff: 1220
Zurich, Muraltengut, Inv. No.4964 (formerly
Benjamin Sharpe, Hanwell Park, Middlesex;
G. & L. Bollag, Zurich; H. Trueb-Baumann,
Hauterive; Max G. Bollag, Zurich)

The following verses from *Oberon* are illustrated
here:

'Oh, fly, sir! or your life's not worth a song!' –
Sir Huon strives, indeed, but strives in vain;
The old man speeds in fullest flight amain,
And after him drags Huon's horse along:
O'er stock and stone, thro' bush and brake they
race,
Nor hedge nor ditch impedes their desperate
pace:
Nor ceas'd the wight to scamper, fear-pursu'd,
Till, clear from out the compass of the wood,
They find themselves at last amid an open space.

A tempest, wing'd with lightning, storm and
rain,
O'ertakes our pair: around them midnight
throws
Darkness that hides the world: it peals, cracks,
blows,
As if the uprooted globe would split in twain:
The elements in wild confusion flung,
Each warred with each, as fierce from chaos
sprung.
Yet heard from time to time amid the storm,
The gentle whisper of th' aërial form
Breath'd forth a lovely tone that died the gales
among –

**138 Titania Shows Amanda her New-born Son
in the Grotto** (1804–5)
(Wieland, *Oberon*, VIII, 75)
Sketch for the engraving by C. Warren in
Oberon, A Poem from the German of Wieland,
by William Sotheby, Esq. (2nd edition),
London 1805

Oil on canvas, 61 × 45 cm
Exh: Zurich 1926 (30); 1941 (28); London
1950 (14); Bremen/Dusseldorf 1957 (19);
Zurich 1969 (83)
Lit: Federmann 1927, pl.19; Jaloux 1942,
p.147
Schiff: 1225
Zurich, Muraltengut, Inv. No.4965 (formerly
Benjamin Sharpe, Hanwell Park, Middlesex;
G. & L. Bollag, Zurich; H. Trueb-Baumann,
Hauterive; Max G. Bollag, Zurich)

136

137

138

139

139a

140

The verse illustrated here is:

> One pulse-beat more – and how divinely great
> At once her mingled wonder and delight –
> She feels, she sees, yet trusts nor sense nor sight,
> She feels herself delivered from her weight,
> While in her lap a quivering infant lies,
> More beauteous than e'er blest a mother's eyes;
> Fresh as a morning rose, and fair as love –
> And, oh! what thrills her swelling bosom move,
> While soft she feels her heart against him fondly rise.

139 Titania Finds the Magic Ring on the Beach
(1804–5)
(Wieland, *Oberon*, X, 2–3)
Engraved by J. Heath in *Oberon, A Poem from the German of Wieland*, by William Sotheby, Esq. (2nd Edition) London 1805

Oil on canvas, 61 × 45 cm
Exh: Zurich 1926 (32); 1941 (29); Paris 1948 (110); Geneva 1948 (194); London 1950 (15); Bremen/Dusseldorf 1957 (20); Zurich 1969 (84)
Lit: Jaloux 1942, p.148; Woodward 1950, p.111; Tomory 1972, repr. 111
Schiff: 1226
Zurich, Kunsthaus (formerly Benjamin Sharpe, Hanwell Park, Middlesex)

Fuseli has borrowed Titania's pose from Blake's illustration to Edward Young's *Night Thoughts*, V, 246: 'I dive for precious pearls in Sorrow's Stream'. It depicts a pearl diver seizing two pearls from the bottom of the sea (cf. Schiff, II, repr. p.384). One of the few examples in Fuseli's work that back up his reputed comment that Blake was 'd---d good to steal from'.

The verses illustrated here are:

> Titania hears him, wrapt in misty air,
> From the far wood in long deep pauses sigh:
> She sees the wretch in silent anguish die,
> And weeps, and flies away in mute despair.
> In vain she ventures near – a viewless hand
> Still drives her back – yet, as she leaves the shore,
> Her last long look that rolls the island o'er
> Darts on a ring of gold that glitters on the sand.
> Reft from Amanda's hand, the ring unseen
> Dropt as she struggled with the pirate train;
> And as Titania seizes it again,
> How beat the bosom of the fairy queen!
> 'Hail! talisman! by elf and spright ador'd!
> Soon shall our fate be full, to love restor'd
> We shall again one nuptial promise plight!
> This once united, shall again unite,
> And crown thee, O belov'd! once more my sov'reign lord!'

140 Almansaris Visits Huon in Prison (1804–5)
(Wieland, *Oberon*, XII, 32–38)
Engraved by J. Heath in *Oberon, A Poem
from the German of Wieland*, by William
Sotheby, Esq. (2nd Edition) London 1805

Oil on canvas, 61 × 45 cm
Exh: Zurich 1926 (33); 1941 (31); Paris 1948
(109); Geneva 1948 (193); Bremen/Dusseldorf
1957 (22); Zurich 1969 (86)
Lit: Boase 1959, p.7, repr. 3b
Schiff: 1228
Zurich, Kunsthaus

Wieland characterises the Sultaness Almansaris first
and foremost as a passionate lover. In this scene she
encounters Huon in the same cruel, threatening
manner as Dalila approaches Samson (cf. No.106)
and Kriemhild approaches Gunther or Hagen (cf.
Nos.145, 147).

The scene illustrated describes Almansaris' entry
into the prison:
When half the world lay wrapt in sleepless night,
A jarring sound the startled hero wakes:
with grating keys the dungeon hoarsely shakes,
The iron door expands: a paly light
Gleams through the vaults, at distance dim
descried:
He hears a step draw near – in beauty's pride
A female comes – wide floats her glistening gown,
Her hand sustains a lamp, her head a crown:
Lo! the sultana's self stands graceful at his side!

Towards the end of her visit Almansaris turned on
Huon as described in the following verses:

But more inflam'd, the more exalted truth
And virtue strengthen his heroick heart,
The wily wanton tries each subtile art,
To bend the spirit of the unconquered youth.
Now lures, now threatens, falls his feet before:
What rage and love suggest, tries o'er and o'er,
In madd'ning passion lost – yet nothing gains.
His steadfast soul immoveable remains,
True to the vow that love to chaste Amanda
swore.

'Die! since thou wilt,' she cries with breathless
ire,
'I, I will stand in triumph o'er thy pile
And on thy death-pang feast my scornful smile!
Victim of sullen pride! dull fool! expire!'
She speaks, and curses loud the luckless hour
When first she felt his fascinating power.
Wild foams her lip, her eyes like lightning glare,
She flies away in merciless despair,
And stern behind her locks the hoarse-resounding
tower.

141 Undine Comes to the Fisherman's Hut [1821]
(Friedrich de la Motte-Fouqué, *Undine*, 2)

Oil on canvas, 73 × 63 cm
Exh: Zurich 1926 (48); 1941 (73); 1969 (104);
Paris 1948 (125); Geneva 1948 (215); London
1950 (26)
Lit: catalogue note to 101, 1947; Antal 1956,
p.138; Photiades 1964, repr. 158; Tomory
1972, pl.XIII, p.182
Schiff: 1499
Basle, Öffentliche Kunstsammlung, Inv. No.1895

The fairytale *Undine*, published in 1811, derives
from a section on elemental spirits in the writings of
the fifteenth-century German Swiss philosopher
and physician, Paracelsus. A fisherman and his wife
have lost their daughter by drowning. Undine, a
capricious watersprite, has inexplicably come to
them and been brought up as their own daughter. A
knight, Huldbrand von Ringstetten, seeks shelter in
their hut and falls in love with Undine. They marry,
and Undine receives a soul. But the other watersprites, especially her uncle Kühleborn, disrupt the
peace of the young married couple. Huldbrand begins to neglect Undine and starts paying attention
to the arrogant Bertalda, who is humiliated to dis-
cover that she is the lost daughter of the fisherman.
While boating on the Danube Undine is snatched
back by the watersprites. Huldbrand decides to
marry Bertalda; but on the morning of the wedding
Undine steps out of a fountain, goes to Huldbrand's
chamber and kisses him, at which he dies.

**142 Brunhild Watching Gunther Suspended from
the Ceiling** 1807
(*Nibelungenlied*, X, 648–50)
Pencil, ink and wash, 48.3 × 31.7 cm
Inscr. bottom right: Πρυνιλδ. Γυνθερ;
above, on the pillar: 'May 1807'
Exh: Bordeaux, *Bosch, Goya et le fantastique*,
1957 (60); Zurich 1959 (41)
Schiff: 1381
Nottingham, Castle Museum, Inv. No. '90-133
(formerly Felix Joseph and Dr John Percy)

This scene from the wedding night of the Burgun-
dian king and queen has never been illustrated by
any other artist. Fuseli gives the triumphant Brunhild the pose of David's 'Madame Récamier'.

Gunther and Brunhild have celebrated their marriage but when Gunther manifests his love for Brunhild she binds his hands and feet and leaves him
hanging upside down so that she may sleep undis-
turbed. Fuseli illustrates Gunther's words:
To mine house a very demon I have brought for
wedding dame!
When I thought to embrace her, swiftly my
limbs into bonds she flung:
To an iron staple she bore me, and against the
wall she hung
There swung I sore in torment the long night
through till the day.
(Arthur S. Way, *The Lay of the Nibelung Men*, 1911)

141

142

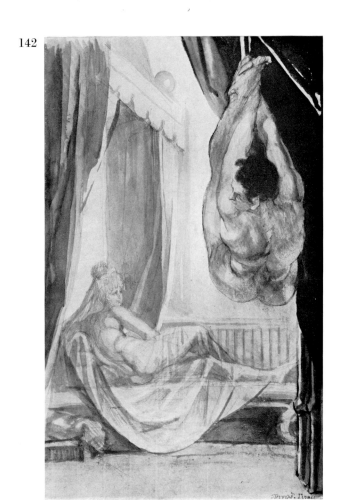

143 Kriemhild Sees Siegfried Dead in a Dream

[1805]

(*Nibelungenlied*, XVI, 935)

Pencil, watercolour and body colour,
38.5 × 48.5 cm
Exh: Zurich 1926 (269); 1941 (166); 1969
(244); London 1950 (108); New York 1954
(10); Bremen/Dusseldorf 1957 (128)
Lit: Beutler, p.19, with repr.; Tomory 1972,
p.182, repr. 116
Schiff: 1385
Zurich, Kunsthaus, Inv. No.1916/18

Kriemhild dreams that Siegfried will be killed. He
pays no heed to her warnings and goes hunting.
While he is out hunting he is murdered by Hagen.

**144 Kriemhild Accuses Gunther and Hagen of
the Murder of Siegfried 1805**

(*Nibelungenlied*, XVII, 152–80)

Pen and wash over pencil, incomplete at top
left, 36.5 × 47.0 cm
Inscr. on left: 'P.C. aug.ᵗ 05'; on the back
stamp of the Countess of Guilford.
Exh: Zurich 1926 (269); 1941 (166); 1969
(246); Bremen/Dusseldorf 1957 (128)
Schiff: 1387
Zurich, Kunsthaus, Inv. No.1914/40 (formerly
Arnold Otto Meyer, Hamburg).

In spite of Kriemhild's entreaties, Siegfried went
hunting. Kriemhild's forebodings were realised and
Siegfried was murdered by Hagen. His father, King
Siegmund, swore to avenge his death. Siegfried's
body was laid on a bier and carried in procession to
the cathedral. Here Kriemhild announced that as
the mourners stood by the dead man's side their
innocence might be proved. But when the murderer
stood close to the body the wounds would once
again start to bleed. In this way, Hagen's guilt was
shown. Gunther hastened to declare Hagen innocent
but Kriemhild accused Gunther and Hagen of plan-
ning Siegfried's death.

**145 The Nymphs of the Danube warn Hagen of the
Unhappy Outcome of Gunther's Expedition to
Kriemhild and Etzel 1802**

(*Nibelungenlied*, XXV, 1577–91)

Pencil, ink, watercolour, heightened with
white, 31.2 × 33.6 cm
Inscr. bottom right: 'Augᵗ 1802'
Exh: Bremen/Dusseldorf 1957 (130)
Lit: Federmann 1927, p.68; Ganz 1947, p.77;
Lankheit 1951, p.179
Schiff: 1392
*New Orleans, Louisiana, Dr and Mrs Richard W.
Levy* (formerly Dr Rudolf Ganz, Paul Ganz,
Oberhofen)

The figure of the ghostlike old woman in the reeds
does not appear in the original text; it is also missing
in Fuseli's painting of the theme (No.126)

143

146 Kriemhild, Accompanied by Two Hun Servants, Shows the Imprisoned Hagen the Ring of the Nibelungen 1807

Watercolour over pencil, 50 × 38.4 cm
Inscr. bottom right: 'Sept. 1807'; on the back, collection stamp of the Countess of Guilford
Exh: Zurich 1926 (251); 1941 (162); 1969 (249); Bremen/Dusseldorf 1957 (133)
Lit: Mandach 1946, p.32
Schiff: 1396
Zurich, Kunsthaus, Inv. No.1940/192 (on loan from the Gottfried Keller Foundation) (formerly Arnold Otto Meyer, Hamburg)

This scene is an interpolation by Fuseli; it does not occur in the original text. Its similarity to No.147 and the presence of the Mongolian servants permit the conclusion that the woman depicted here is also Kriemhild. In the *Nibelungenlied* Hagen stole the Nibelungen gold from her and sank it in the Rhine near Lochheim (XIX Adventure). In the songs in the *Edda* about the Nibelungen, the most important part of the treasure is the ring 'Andwaranaut', which has the power to increase the gold infinitely. This ring does not feature in the *Nibelungenlied*. Fuseli seems to conjecture that this ring must also have belonged to the treasure in the *Nibelungenlied* and that Hagen gave it to Gunther. When she had Gunther killed, Kriemhild took the ring off his finger. The ring brings death to all who wear it. So she shows it to Hagen to inform him of Gunther's death, and is about to give it to him as a means of warning him of his own imminent death. The magical power of the ring is suggested by the rays of light radiating from it. Hagen shrinks back in horror showing that he is aware of its implication.

144

147 Kriemhild Shows Hagen Gunther's head 1805
(*Nibelungenlied*, XXXIX, 2440)

Pencil and grey wash, 48.8 × 38.7 cm
Inscr. bottom right: 'P.[urser's] Cr.[oss] 10 Jun. 05'
Exh: Zurich 1926 (272); 1941 (168); 1969 (248); Bremen/Dusseldorf 1957 (131)
Lit: Mandach 1946, p.33, 42, repr. p.41
Schiff: 1395.
Zurich, Kunsthaus, Inv. No.1940/193 (on loan from the Gottfried Keller Foundation)

Kriemhild wants to recover the treasure from Hagen. Hagen has sworn not to reveal its whereabouts while any of the princes are alive. Kriemhild therefore commands her servants to kill her brother, Gunther, the last surviving prince. She holds up his head as proof of his death.

145

146

147

148 The Discovery [1767–9]

Pen and sepia wash, 52.5 × 65.7 cm
Schiff: 336
Chicago, Art Institute (formerly Countess of
Guilford; Arthur Crossland; Durlacher Bros;
Frank B. Hubachek)

This drawing illustrates a story recounted by
Erasmus of Rotterdam in a letter written in Basle
in September 1528 to an unnamed bishop (cf.
Epistolarum D. Erasmi Roterodami Libri XXXI . . .
London 1642, p.1186ff.). The story is repeated almost
word for word in the Zurich theologian Ludwig
Lavater's treatise on ghosts (*De Spectris*, Zurich
1750, I, chap.IX) which Fuseli had in his library.
This book had some influence on his attitude to be-
lief in ghosts and his choice of such themes.

Erasmus describes a priest who, wrapped in a
sheet and making ambiguous noises, used to pay
nocturnal visits to a wealthy niece living in his
house. One night the girl called out to a relative,
who challenged the apparition with the words: 'If
you are the devil, I am his grandmother' and all but
clubbed him to death. At this the 'ghost' revealed
his identity; 'I am not the devil, but Dominus Jo-
hannes'. On recognising his voice the niece sprang
out of bed and stopped the fight.

The shuttlecock players in the courtyard visible
beyond the chamber do not feature in the story.

149 The Faerie Queene Appears to Prince Arthur
[*c.*1769]
(Edmund Spenser, *The Faerie Queene*, I, IX, 13)

Pen and watercolour with white highlights
38.2 × 50 cm; on the back a red chalk sketch
of the Faerie Queene and Prince Arthur
Exh: Zurich 1969 (120)
Lit: Ganz 1947, 9; Antal 1956, p.20, p.104
Schiff: 337
Berne, Private collection

In this drawing Fuseli goes back to an obvious
iconographic tradition, namely the scene from Tas-
so's *Gerusalemme Liberata* (XVI, p.65ff.) so often
painted by Baroque artists. It describes the enchan-
tress Armida binding Rinaldo, who has fallen asleep
by the banks of the Orontes, with a garland of flowers. Fuseli's immediate source of inspiration was
probably Van Dyck's version of the theme (*c.*1627,
now in Los Angeles) which at that time was in the
possession of the Earl of Fitzwilliam at Wentworth
House in Yorkshire. Both Fuseli's and Van Dyck's
representations go back ultimately to the theme of
Selene appearing to the sleeping Endymion on
Endymion sarcophagi; like the Faerie Queene she
wears a billowing circular cloak. In Spenser's poem
the meeting of Arthur and Gloriana (who also represents Elizabeth, the virgin queen) is an allegory
of a great soul inflamed with lofty aims. Fuseli's
depiction tends to emphasize the erotic fascination
rather than the allegorical content. Also, by intro-

ducing the sprites he transfers the whole scene to the more earthbound sphere of traditional fairy tales.

The lines illustrated are as follows:

For – wearied with my sports, I did alight
From loftiesteed, and down to sleepe me layd;
The verdant gras did goodly dight,
And pillow was my helmet faire displayed:
Whiles every sence the humour sweet embayd,
And slombring soft my hart did steale away,
Me seemed by my side a royall Mayd.
Her daintie limbs full softly down did lay:
So faire a creature yet saw never sunny day.

150 The Cave of Despair [*c.*1769]
(Edmund Spenser, *The Faerie Queene*, I, IX, 21–54)

Pen and sepia wash, 33 × 50.5 cm
Lit: Middledorf 1946, p.425; Erffa 1947, p.106f.
Schiff: 338
Chicago, Art Institute, Leonora Hall Gurley
Memorial Collection

Despair, the demon of religious melancholy, broods over the corpse of a man who has stabbed himself to death. Another youth has just managed to escape from Despair's insinuations; with the noose still round his neck, he glances back into the cave. Redcrosse, the personification of piety, draws his sword at the demon. But he too will later succumb to the suggestion of death. Only his companion Una, the sole Christian truth, will be able to save him with her theological arguments.

148

149

150

151

151 Malengin Flees from Arthegall, Arthur Guards his Cave [1795–1800]
(Edmund Spenser, *The Faerie Queene*, V, IX, XV)

Pencil, pen and ink with sepia wash,
40.5 × 32.1 cm
Exh: Zurich 1941 (368); London 1950 (103);
New York 1954 (52); Bremen/Dusseldorf
1957 (110); Zurich 1969 (193)
Lit: Ganz 1947, 74; Hofmann 1952, p.169
Schiff: 1007
Zurich, Kunsthaus, Inv. No.1938/632
(Ganz Bequest)

The fifth book of *The Faerie Queene* deals with justice, personified by Sir Arthegall, who in turn stands for Lord Grey de Wilton whom Spenser accompanied on his expedition to Ireland in 1580. Though the book presents, amongst other things, a justification of Queen Elizabeth's imperialist policies, justice here is paradoxically exemplified by Lord Grey's extermination of the Irish rebels. Sir Arthur, 'maganimity', assists him in this. Malengin represents the courageous guerillas. In another version (Schiff 1006) Fuseli follows the text precisely. Here, on the other hand, he seems to have simply used the figures to enliven his sketch of 'Caves in the Cliffs near Margate' drawn from memory (cf. No.201)

152

152 Pastoral Scene (I) [*c*.1777–8]

Pen and ink, 23.3 × 19 cm
Schiff: 488
London, Trustees of the British Museum,
Roman Album, fol.3V, No.1,
Inv. No. 1885-3-14-201

This composition was possibly inspired by the following lines from Salomon Gessner's Idyllen, where Daphnis tells Chloe:

Chloe, as I looked at my reflection in the quiet
pool, Ah, I sighed, could I but please Daphnis,
the best shepherd. Meanwhile, unknown to me,
you stood behind and threw flowers over my
head into the pool, so that my image vanished
in the swirling circles. Shocked, I turned round...
(*Gessners Schriften*, III, Zurich 1765, p.59; reference by Prof. R.E. Straub, Stuttgart)

153

153 Pastoral Scene (II) [*c*.1777–8]

Pen and ink, 18.9 × 24.2 cm
Schiff: 489
London, Trustees of the British Museum,
Roman Album, fol.3V, No.2,
Inv. No.1885-3-14-202

The girl has been transformed into an elegant rococo lady lying on her side with her arms resting on a square stone.

154 **The Devil Comes for the Sompnour and the Frying Pan the Latter had Taken from the Widow whom he Deceitfully Accused of Adultery** 1821
(Geoffrey Chaucer, *The Canterbury Tales – The Friar's Tale*, 7153–7226)

Pencil and wash, partially outlined in ink, 40.6 × 32.2 cm
Inscr. bottom right: 'P.H. [Putney Hill] 8 July – 21'; on the back, collection stamp of the Countess of Guilford
Exh: Zurich 1969 (287)
Lit: Tomory 1972, repr. 161, p.127
Schiff: 1567
Zurich, Graphische Sammlung der Eidgenössischen Technischen Hochschule
Inv. No.1935/42

155 **Undine Comes to the Fisherman's Hut** 1821
(Friedrich de la Motte-Fouqué, *Undine*, ch. 2)

Pencil, 32.1 × 40.7 cm
Inscr. bottom left: 'P.H. 14 May – 21';
Watermark 'Snelgrove & Son 1820'
Exh: Zurich 1941 (456); 1969 (282)
Schiff: 1560
Zurich, Kunsthaus, Inv. No.1940/56

A study for the painting, No.141.

The old fisherman tells how Undine came to live with him and his wife. Late in life they had a daughter who was drowned one day as she played beside the lake in the park. He continues:

> Well, the same evening, we two desolate parents were sitting silently in the cottage; we had no wish to talk, even if we could have done so for our tears. We sat gazing into the flame upon the hearth. Then came a noise of something rattling at the door: it opened, and a marvellously lovely little maid of three or four years stood in a rich dress, on the threshold, and smiled at us. We were stricken quite dumb with astonishment, and at first I could not be sure whether it was a real little human being or merely a delusive vision. Then I perceived that water was dripping from the golden hair and the rich raiment and saw that the lovely child had fallen into the water and needed help. (E. Gosse)

156 **Undine Displeased Leaves the Fisherman's Hut** 1822
(Friedrich de la Motte-Fouqué, *Undine*, chs. 1–2)

Pencil with blue and grey wash, 32.0 × 37.6 cm
Inscr: 'Petersham Augst 19 Putney Hill 5 May 22'
Exh: Zurich 1926 (341); 1941 (177); 1969 (283); London 1950 (133); Bremen/Dusseldorf 1956 (153)

Lit: Ganz 1947, 105–6; Lankheit 1951, p.180; Antal 1956, p.141ff., pl.60a; Schiff 1960 (2), pp.71–6; Tomory 1972, repr. 146, p.126
Schiff: 1563
Zurich, Kunsthaus, Inv. No.1938/631 (Ganz Bequest)

While the fisherman was sitting at the door of his cottage, mending his nets, a handsome knight appeared on horseback. The fisherman led the knight into his cottage where his wife was sitting by the fire. While they talked, they were disturbed by the old couple's fosterdaughter, Undine. The knight marvelled at her beauty. Undine bombarded him with questions but was scolded by her foster-parents. The drawing illustrates the following lines:

> He loudly reproved Undine for her disobedience and her rude behaviour in the presence of the visitor; and the old wife joined in. Then Undine said: 'If you are going to scold me, and do nothing as I wish it done, then sleep by yourselves in your smoky old cottage.' And like an arrow she shot out of the door and vanished into the darkness of the night.
> Huldbrand the knight and the fisherman leaped from their seats and prepared to pursue the angry girl. (E. Gosse)

157

157 Kuhleborn startles Bertalda [1819–22]
(Friedrich de la Motte-Fouqué, *Undine*, ch.13)

Pencil and black chalk with watercolour, 32.2 × 20.6 cm. The contours of the drawing have been traced through onto the reverse.
Watermark 'Golding & Snelgrove 1818'
Exh: Zurich 1941 (446); 1969 (284); New York 1954 (61); Bremen/Dusseldorf 1957 (150)
Lit: Ganz 1947, 101–2
Schiff: 1564
Zurich, Kunsthaus, Inv. No.1940/19 (formerly Paul Hürlimann)

Undine and Huldbrand, now married, journeyed back to the city where Huldbrand's first love, Bertalda, was living with her foster-parents. Here it was discovered that Bertalda is the long-lost daughter of the fisherman and his wife. Undine and Bertalda went with Huldbrand to his home, Ringstetten Castle. While they were staying there Huldbrand fell in love again with Bertalda. The drawing illustrates the following lines:

> Undine gave way in melancholy resignation, and which was usually supported in the firmest manner by the infatuated Huldbrand. What still further disturbed social life in the castle were all sorts of strange apparitions, which confronted Huldbrand and Bertalda in the vaulted passages of the fortress . . . The tall white man, in whom, only too well Huldbrand recognised (Undine's) Uncle Kühleborn, and Bertalda the ghostly fountain-man, often rose menacingly before them

158

NORTHERN POETS AND LEGENDS

both, but particularly in front of Bertalda, so that already once or twice she had been made quite ill with the terror of it, and often determined that she would quit the castle. (E. Gosse)

158 The Ghost of Undine Emerging from the Well
[1819–22]
(Friedrich de la Motte-Fouqué, *Undine*, ch.18)
Pencil, pen and ink with a light sepia wash, 41.0 × 32.1 cm
Watermark 'Golding & Snelgrove 1818'
Exh: Zurich 1941 (447); 1969 (285); Bremen/Dusseldorf 1957 (149)
Lit: Ganz 1947, Nos.102–3; Lankheit 1951, p.180; Antal 1954, p.95; Schiff 1964, p.134, repr. 92
Schiff: 1565
Zurich, Kunsthaus, Inv. No.1940/21 (formerly Paul Hürlimann)

Undine, Bertalda and Huldbrand journeyed along the river Danube to Vienna. While they were making their way along the river, Undine disappeared over the side of the boat. Back again at Ringstetten Castle, Huldbrand decided to marry Bertalda. During the wedding party Bertalda had the stone slab removed from the fountain which Undine had some time ago insisted should be placed there. The lines illustrated are:

The men heaved with all their strength at the great slab. Now and then one would sigh at the thought that the work of their dear late mistress was being undone. But the toil proved really much less than might have been supposed. It seemed as though a force within the fountain was helping them to lift the stone . . . And the stone rose higher and higher and almost without help from the labourers it slowly rolled with a dull thud upon the pavement. But at the same moment there rose from the opening of the fountain a white pillar of water high into the air. At first they thought that it really had turned into a spring until they noticed that the soaring stream took the shape of a pale woman veiled in white. It wept bitterly, it wrung its hands in anguish about its head, and slowly, slowly it stepped towards the castle building. The castle servants started back from the fountain; the bride stood, pale and stark with terror . . . When the figure was close underneath her chamber it gazed plaintively at her, and Bertalda fancied that beneath the veil she could perceive the pale lineaments of Undine. (E. Gosse)

Women

159 The Nightmare [1781]

Oil on canvas, 101 × 127 cm
Repr: engravings by Laurede, 1782; T. Burke,
1783; de Ville Neuve, 1784; W. Raddon, 1827
Exh: London, Royal Academy, 1781; London,
Roland, Browse & Delbanco, 1948 (25); New
York, Durlacher Bros., *Romanticism in
Eighteenth Century England*, Jan-Feb 1953;
Kansas City, Mo., William Rockhill Nelson
Art Gallery and Hartford, Conn., Wadsworth
Atheneum, Jan-Apr. 1956, *The Century of
Mozart*; Columbus, Ohio, Columbus Gallery of
Fine Arts, *Romantic Painting, Romantic
Prints*, 1963 (15); Zurich, 1969 (25)
Lit: Huber 1802, p.280; Dayes 1805, p.327;
Horner 1826, p.10; Anon. 1826, p.110; Cun-
ningham 1830, p.277; Knowles 1831, I, p.64;
Haydon 1853, II, p.90; Haydon 1960–63, III,
p.14; Thornbury 1860, p.135; Timbs 1860,
p.189ff.; Dafforne 1861, p.325; Sandby 1862,
I, p.207; Muther 1903, pp.91, 94; Schmid 1904,
I, p.55; Gurlitt 1900, p.39ff.; Michel 1919, p.28;
Pauli 1925, p.135; Federmann 1927, p.51;
Denk 1930, pp.114, 122; Ganz 1947, p.14ff.,
65ff.; Redgrave 1947, p.114; *Apollo*, March
1950, p.61; Powell 1951, p.16; Mason 1951,
pp.63, 70, 79, 80; Praz 1952, p.62; Richardson
1954–5, p.2ff. (repr.); Kaiser 1957, p.213, note
20; Brion 1960, p.39; Solier 1961, p.142; Schiff
1960, p.25; Janson 1963, p.23ff.; Irwin 1966,
p.44; Rosenblum 1966, p.176; Klingender
1968, p.16ff., repr. 26–7; Schneck 1969,
p.725ff., repr. in colour; Tomory 1972, pl.l,
pp.31, 33, 92ff., 183, 201
Schiff: 757/759
Detroit, The Detroit Institute of Art (formerly
Haskett Smith)

A sleeping girl whose head and arms are hanging
over the end of the bed is haunted by the incubus
seated on the pit of her stomach. The 'nightmare'
on which an incubus travels sticks its head through
the bed hangings. On the back of the canvas is the
portrait of a young woman. According to H.W.
Janson, the depiction of the nightmare may be a

projection of Fuseli's unfulfilled passion for Anna Landolt, in which case it might well be her portrait on the back of the canvas. Anna Landolt was a niece of Lavater's, and was twenty-one years old when Fuseli met her during his stay in Zurich between October 1778 and April 1779. He fell passionately in love and seriously wanted to marry her. When her father turned down his suit, he returned to London; but even there 'Nanna' continued to dominate his inflamed passionate desires. On 16 June 1779 he wrote to Lavater describing how he had made love with her in his dreams the previous night. One explanation for Fuseli's repeated depiction of the nightmare theme could be that it had a specific, deep meaning for him; namely, that his jealousy and repressed love for Anna Landolt, in the mean time married to another man, haunted her in the form of unpleasant dreams.

159v

160 An Incubus Leaving Two Sleeping Girls
[c.1793]

Oil on canvas, 100 × 124 cm
Exh: Bremen/Dusseldorf 1957 (4); Zurich 1969 (57)
Lit: Schiff 1965, p.110ff., repr. 121
Schiff: 929; cf. No.168
Zurich, Muraltengut, Inv. No.2751

161 Titania's Dream [1790–1800]

Oil on canvas, 79 × 61 cm
Exh: Zurich 1969 (53)
Schiff: 923
La-Tour-de-Peilz, Edouard M. Sandoz
(formerly Maurice Sandoz)

Despite the fact that the study for this painting (Schiff 1080) is traditionally known as 'Titania's Dream', it actually depicts a fashionable scene with Fuseli's characteristic addition of elements from fairy mythology. It is not based on any literary precedent.

160

162 The Ladies of Hastings
[1798–1800; after 1813?]

Oil on canvas, 111 × 80 cm
Inscr. on contemporary frame: 'The Ladies of Hastings'; signed on the stretcher in pencil: 'Vision at Margate S.N. – opposite Window on Landing – end of Study nr Billiard room door'; and a sticker with the name Lord Harrowby Stafford on it (since removed)
Exh: Zurich 1926 (52); 1936 (23); 1941 (21); Paris 1948 (107); Geneva 1948 (191); London 1950 (12); Bremen/Dusseldorf 1957 (16); Zurich 1969 (55)
Lit: *Atlantis*, February 1941 (repr.); Gradmann/Cetto 1944, p.75; Ganz 1947, p.68, No.60; Harcourt-Smith 1950, p.77; Antal 1956, p.120ff., repr. 50; Tomory 1972, repr. 143

161

162

Schiff: 927
Zurich, Private collection
(formerly Lady Susan North, Earl of
Harrowby, Stafford)

Neither date nor meaning of this painting are documented. The clothes worn by the ladies on the sand
dunes are the same as the fashions worn by Mrs
Fuseli in the portraits executed between 1798 and
1800. The inscription 'Vision at Margate' on the
stretcher is in Lady Susan North's handwriting.
Fuseli was in Margate in 1792, but the fashions and
hairstyles depicted rule out any date as early as that.
The alternatives are as follows: either to assume
that in the late 1790s he took up and developed a
theme that had first struck him in Margate in 1792,
and that either he or someone else gave it its present
title at a later date; or else we link it with a stay in
Hastings in 1813, and interpret the outmoded fashions as a deliberate return to an earlier period of his
life, which would not be incompatible with the nature of a vision. On the back of a drawing of cliffs
on the South Coast (No.206), presumably executed
in Margate, there is a sketch of three women in billowing dresses climbing down the dunes. Whether it
is a record of a vision or a scene he actually observed,
it was clearly the starting point for 'The Ladies of
Hastings'. Fuseli must have largely invented the
composition he constructed out of this initial
sketch; there is no known local folk tale of 'The
Ladies of Hastings.' In the preliminary sketch
(No.173), the youth at the bottom of the dune can
be identified by the spade and pile of earth beside
the hole as a digger for hidden treasure; the naked
pointing figure and the storm brewing up in the sky
behind the women are omitted. The treasure hunter
is the witness of a procession of women, possibly
taken from life, though their fans are somewhat
strange. In the final picture all traces of the treasure
hunter have vanished and one has the impression
the ladies are supernatural beings – Fuseli always
dressed his fairies in contemporary clothes – usher-
ing in a storm on the orders of some elementary
godhead. In folklore the hurricane was personified
by demonic females like Diana, the wild huntress,
or Herodias, condemned to dance for all eternity;
in German mythology the giant Fasolt commands
the storms.

163v

163 A Nude Reclining and a Woman Playing
the Piano [1799–1800] (colour repr. p.28)

Oil on canvas, 71 × 91 cm
On the back: Three Courtesans
Exh: Zurich 1969 (54)
Lit: Antal 1956, p.102, repr. 42; Gradmann/
Cetto 1944, p.74, repr. 66 back; Todd 1946,
frontispiece
Schiff: 925/926
Basle, Öffentliche Kunstsammlung (formerly
Ambassador Dr Anton Roy Ganz, Lausanne)

164

165

The disposition of the figures in the 'Nude Reclining and a Woman Playing the Piano' is reminiscent of Titian's 'Venus and the Organ Player' (*c*.1545–50, versions in Berlin and Madrid).

164 Woman at the Window by Moonlight
[1800–10]

Oil on canvas, 71 × 92.5 cm
Exh: Zurich 1936 (20); 1941 (50); Paris 1948
(114); Geneva 1948 (198); Zurich 1969 (95)
Lit: Beutler 1955, p.19
Schiff: 1240
Frankfurt am Main, Goethe-Museum
(formerly Paul Ganz)

165 Portrait of Mrs Fuseli [*c*.1792]

Oil on canvas, in oval frame, 73.3 × 62.3 cm
Schiff: 930
London, Private collection (formerly Mr
Thomas Lowinsky)

166 Portrait of Mrs Otway Cave [1820–25]

Oil on canvas, 91.5 × 71.1 cm
Exh: Zurich 1969 (109)
Lit: Mason 1951 (2), p.9, note 1; p.10, note 1;
Antal 1956
Schiff: 1506
Berne, Private collection

Mrs Otway Cave (1794–1849) was the daughter of Sir Francis Burdett, the campaigner for electoral reform, and his wife Sophia, the youngest daughter of the banker Coutts, Fuseli's patron. In 1833 she married the Irish landowner Otway Cave. The Zurich Kunsthaus possesses nineteen letters and notes written by the octogenarian Fuseli to the young Sophia Burdett.

166

167 The Changeling 1780

Pencil and watercolour, 48 × 53.5 cm
Inscr. 'London March 80'
Exh: Zurich 1969 (180)
Lit: Ganz 1947 (39)
Schiff: 840
Zurich, Kunsthaus, Inv. No.1940/139
(formerly Paul Hürlimann)

After a fairy abducts a child, its mother finds in the cradle an ugly changeling that has been substituted while the old nurse was asleep.

168 The Incubus Leaving Two Sleeping Women
1810

Pencil and watercolour, 31.5 × 40.8 cm
Inscr. bottom left in Greek (Homer, *Iliad*, X,
496 ff.): ασθμαίνυσαν κακὸν γὰρ ὸναξ
κεφαλῆσιν ἐπέστη τῆν νύκτ'
'As he breathed hard, for like to an evil dream
there stood above his head that night . . .'
(A.T. Murray); on the right: 'Q[ueens] E[lm]
may 28. 10. June 4'

167

168

Exh: Zurich 1926 (280); 1941 (172); Paris
1948 (145); Geneva 1948 (238); London 1950
(11); Bremen/Dusseldorf 1954 (140)
Lit: Ganz 1947, 84; Harcourt-Smith 1950,
p.77; Antal 1956, p.102, pl.45b
Schiff: 1445; cf. No.160
Zurich, Kunsthaus, Inv. No.1914/26 (formerly
Arnold Otto Meyer, Hamburg)

169

169 Bathing Scene [1800–05]

Pen and ink and wash, 15.5 × 28 cm
Exh: Zurich 1926 (182); 1941 (325); 1969
(255); Paris 1948 (135); Geneva 1948 (228);
New York 1954 (46); Bremen/Dusseldorf 1957
(58); St. Gallen, *Malende Dichter – Dichtende
Maler* (Painting Poets – Poeticising Painters),
1957 (236)
Lit: Ganz 1947, No.50; Antal 1956, p.96
Schiff: 1401
Zurich, Kunsthaus, Inv. No.1916/23

Ganz's often repeated interpretation of this scene as
'The Fall of Icarus and bathing Women' seems un-
tenable because the figure springing into the water
is a woman. The erotic overtones in the scene are
undeniable. It appears to have no mythological
derivation. Fuseli possibly had in mind one of the
numerous references in antique and more recent
literature to the Baths of Pozzuoli (Puteolanum) as

a place of great debauchery. (For a synopsis of the most important texts from Varro to Boccaccio cf. C.M. Kauffmann, *The Baths of Pozzuoli*, Oxford 1959, p.1ff.) But Fuseli could also have derived his inspiration from a book by his collector friend, The Rev. William Shepherd, *The Life of Poggio Bracciolini* (1802). In this volume Shepherd prints a letter Poggio wrote to Nicolo Nicoli in 1417 about the baths at Baden in the Aargau which were reputed to surpass even the debauchery at Pozzuoli. Formally, the composition appears to be based on Virgil Solis' engraving after Aldegrever's 'Bath of the Anabaptists' (after 1534, Bartsch, IX, p.277, No.265), which Fuseli owned.

170

170 A Couple Kissing [*c*.1815]

Pencil, 31.6 × 20.4 cm
Exh: Zurich 1941 (418); London 1950 (124);
Bremen/Dusseldorf 1957 (145)
Lit: Federmann 1927, pl.61; Ganz 1947,
99–100; Woodward 1950, p.360; Antal 1956,
p.139, repr. 57b
Schiff: 1583
Basle, Öffentliche Kunstsammlung,
Inv. No.1917.187

171 Nude Woman Seated on Top of a Faintly Sketched Male Body [1810–20]

Pencil, 24.7 × 19.9 cm
On the back: two courtesans maiming a child
Schiff: 1622/1625
Hamburg, Private collection
(formerly Roger P. Senhouse London)

171r

172 Callipyga, a Woman with her Skirt Lifted Standing before a Dressing-table with Phallic Supports [1810–20]

Pen and ink, 16.3 × 9.4 cm
Schiff: 1618
London, Private collection

173 The Ladies of Hastings [1798–1800? or after 1813?]

Pencil, 23 × 18.5 cm
Exh: Zurich 1920 (240); 1941 (347); 1969 (205)
Lit: Ganz 1947, 60
Schiff: 1081
Zurich, Kunsthaus, Inv. No.1938/647
(Ganz Bequest)

Preparatory study for the painting of the same theme, No.162

171v

174 Fear: Three Crouching Girls [*c*.1780–82]

Pencil and white chalk on cardboard,
40.1 × 53.7 cm
On the back some faint figure sketches;
collection stamp of the Countess of Guilford
Exh: Zurich 1926 (164); 1941 (281); London

172

173

174

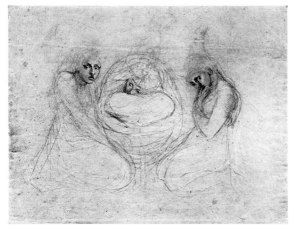

176

175

1950 (65); New York 1954 (36); Zurich 1969
(179)
Lit: Woodward 1950, p.112; Antal 1956, p.92,
139ff., pl.17; Tomory 1972, repr. 64
Schiff: 839
Zurich, Kunsthaus, Inv. No.1940/145
(formerly Paul Hürlimann)

175 Silence [1780–85]

Black chalk, 43 × 29.5 cm
Exh: *William Blake and His Circle,* London,
British Museum, Bicentenary Exhibition,
Lit: Powell 1951 (30); 1957, No.85 (2)
Schiff: 850
London, Trustees of the British Museum,
Inv. No.1907-11-6-3

**176 Magdalena Schweizer-Hess Seen in Profile
from the Right** 1779

Pencil, 48.9 × 33.8 cm
Inscr. bottom left: 'H. Fuseli fec. de. 15
Martii 1779'
Exh: Zurich 1969 (128)
Lit: Federmann 1927, p.51; Schiff: 1964 (2),
p.152, repr. 15
Schiff: 578
Zurich, Zentralbibliothek

**177 Mrs Fuseli, her Hair in Large Rolls, with
Pink Gloves, in front of a Brown Curtain** 1790

Pencil with grey and brown wash heightened
with pink, 21.6 × 19.7 cn
Inscr. bottom right in pencil: 'Dec 90'; on the
back the collection stamp of the Countess of
Guilford
Exh: Zurich 1926 (201); 1941 (180); Paris
1948 (131); Geneva 1948 (224); London 1950
(73); Turin 1951 (159); New York 1954 (19);
Bremen/Dusseldorf 1957 (88); Zurich 1969
(207)
Lit: Federmann 1927, pl.41
Schiff: 1084
Zurich, Kunsthaus, Inv. No.1914/32
(formerly Arnold Otto Meyer, Hamburg)

177

178 Double Portrait of Mrs Fuseli [1791–2]

Pencil with grey wash, 22.2 × 17.8 cm
On the back: 'Two Courtesans at a Window'
Exh: Zurich 1959 (23); 1969 (209)
Lit: Schiff 1959, 23
Schiff: 1093
Belfast, Ulster Museum, Inv. No.3539 (II)
verso

178

179

180

181

179 Mrs Fuseli in a Big Hat [*c.*1792]

Pen and ink, 13.3 × 13.3 cm
Another version on the back
Exh: Zurich 1959 (28)
Lit: Schiff 1959, 28
Schiff: 1053
Belfast, Ulster Museum, Inv. No.3539 (VI)

180 Mrs Fuseli Seated in the Corner of a Sofa, in a Wide-brimmed Hat [1792–1795]

Watercolour, 48 × 31.2 cm
Inscr. at bottom right in Greek letters:
'Restlessly I chased the image of my dream through the passing fashions'
Exh: Zurich 1941 (184); London 1950 (83); Zurich 1969 (214)
Lit: Mandach 1946, p.31
Schiff: 1104
Zurich, Kunsthaus, Inv. No.1934/2 (on loan from the Gottfried Keller Foundation); (formerly Kündig Collection)

181 Mrs Fuseli, her Hair Piled High in Powdered Curls 1796

Pencil, ink, grey and pale pink wash, 28 × 22.3 cm
Inscr. bottom right in sepia ink: '8 Oct.ʳ 96'; below, in an unknown hand: 'by Sir Joshua Reynolds'; on the back, a sepia drawing of a courtesan holding a switch; collection stamp of the Countess of Guilford
Exh: Zurich 1926 (226); 1941 (185); Paris 1948 (136); Geneva 1948 (229); London 1950 (84); Zurich 1969 (215)
Schiff: 1108
Zurich, Kunsthaus, Inv. No.1914/35 (formerly Arnold Otto Meyer, Hamburg)

182 Mrs Fuseli Seated in Front of the Fire, Behind Her a Relief Medallion with her Portrait as the Medusa 1799

Ink and grey wash and watercolour over pencil, 33.6 × 19.9 cm
Inscr. on the frame of the medallion:
ΕΥΠΑΡΑΟΥ ΚΡΑΤΑ ΜΕΔΟΙΣΑΣ
below, on her hem: 'Dec.ʳ 4. 99'
On the back: 'Mrs Fuseli Seated Making a Gesture of Silence'
Exh: Berlin 1906 (2492); Constance 1953 (2)
Lit: Laban 1907, p.11ff., frontispiece; Stengel 1913, p.18ff., repr. 22; Kaesbach/Kurella 1921, repr. p.7; Weinberger 1923, p.30 and pl.32; Heffels 1969, No. 126, p.102f., with repr.
Schiff: 1118
Nuremberg, Germanisches Nationalmuseum, Inv. No.3399a

The quotation comes from Pindar, *Pythians*, 12, 16. Fuseli compares his wife's head and hair-style to 'the head of fair-faced Medusa' (Medusa, who ac-

cording to some legends was a beautiful woman, had her hair transformed into snakes by Athena and anyone who looked on her face was turned into stone.)

183 Profile Portrait of Mrs Fuseli Seated Facing Left, with her Hair Tied Back [1810]

Pencil, ink and wash, 24 × 16.5 cm
Schiff: 1648
London, Victoria and Albert Museum,
Inv. No.8815E

This is one of twelve drawings executed in 1810 in which Fuseli repeated portraits of his wife made between 1794 and 1800. On the basis of her hairstyle and dress the lost original of this portrait probably dated from 1798 (cf. the drawing in Basle dated 8 July 1798, Schiff 1111).

184 Two Girls Looking Upwards out of a Cabin Window 1779

Pencil with sepia wash, 21.7 × 17.3 cm
Inscr. bottom left in pencil: 'Ostende apr. 79'
Exh: Zurich 1926 (151); 1941 (273); Paris 1948 (127); Geneva 1948 (220); London 1950 (53); Bremen/Dusseldorf 1957 (76); Zurich 1969 (154)
Lit: Federmann 1927, pl.64 top; Ganz 1947, 36; Dörries 1943, repr. p.83; Antal 1956, p.44
Schiff: 553
Basle, Öffentliche Kunstsammlung, Inv. No.1914/287

185 Bust of a Girl Looking over her Left Shoulder [1780–1785]

Black chalk, 46 × 30 cm
Inscr. in pencil at bottom: 'which'
On the back: a study of a leg, a portrait of Fuseli by an unknown artist inscribed by an unknown hand: 'large blue Fuseli'
Schiff: 855
Zurich, Graphische Sammlung der Eidgenössischen Technischen Hochschule

186 Woman Seated on a Sofa [1790–92]

Pen, ink, and wash, 18.3 × 20 cm
On the reverse: the figure of a seated woman seen from the back, turning to the left: she has a mass of flame-like curls and is making a pointing gesture
Exh: Zurich 1926 (202); 1941 (238); Bremen/ Dusseldorf 1957 (89)
Lit: Ganz 1947, 52; Praz 1952, p.35 with repr.; Tomory 1972, repr. 188, pp.114, 171
Schiff: 1057
Zurich, Kunsthaus, Inv. No.1913/4

184

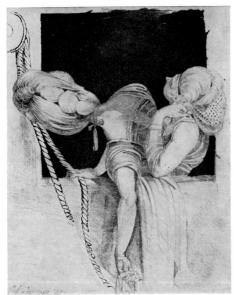

188^r

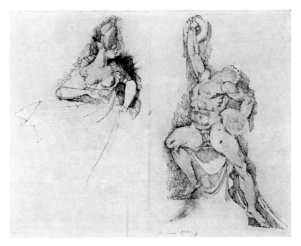

188^v

185

189

186

187 Three Women with Baskets Descending a Staircase [1798–1800]

Pen and sepia ink with wash, 37.5 × 23.2 cm
Exh: Bordeaux, *Bosch, Goya et le fantastique*,
1957 (61); Zurich 1959 (35)
Lit: Schiff 1959, No.35; Tomory 1972, p.169,
repr. 176
Schiff: 1083
Nottingham, Castle Museum, Inv. No.1890/172
(formerly Felix Joseph and Dr John Percy)

Tomory's attempt to attribute this drawing to John Brown appears to be without foundation.

188 A Woman before the Laocoon [1801–5]

Pencil, pen, and ink, 32 × 40.4 cm
On the reverse: another, unfinished version
Watermark 'S & D 1801'
Lit: Federmann 1927, pl.42; Irwin 1966, p.48;
Tomory 1972, repr. 218, p.118
Schiff: 1072
Zurich, Kunsthaus, Inv. No.1913/7

189 Courtesan with Naked Breast, Standing in front of a Fire, Holding a Switch; behind her to the left a Small Crouching Fairy [1800–1805]

Pen and ink over pencil, 31.9 × 20 cm
Exh: Zurich 1941 (191); 1969 (266); Paris
1948 (140); Geneva 1948 (233); London 1950
(97); New York 1954 (24); Bremen/
Dusseldorf 1957 (116)
Lit: Ganz 1947, 62; Lankheit 1951, p.175
Schiff: 1441
Zurich, Kunsthaus, Inv. No.1938/679
(Ganz Bequest)

190 Half-length Figure of a Courtesan with Feathers, a Bow and a Veil in her Hair [1800–1810]

Pencil, watercolour, ink, 28.3 × 20 cm
In the background: a similarly dressed figure
gathering up her dress and pointing into the
distance; on the back: some figure sketches
Exh: Zurich 1941 (183); 1969 (265); Paris 1948
(134); Geneva 1948 (227); London 1950 (82);
Bremen/Dusseldorf 1957 (117)
Lit: Mandach 1946, pp.31, 42, repr. p.35;
Ganz 1947, 81; Lankheit 1951, p.176; Praz
1952, p.34, repr.; Schiff 1960, p.29
Schiff: 1440
Zurich, Kunsthaus, Inv. No.1934/1
(on loan from the Gottfried Keller Foundation;
formerly Countess of Guilford)

187

190

191 The Debutante 1807

> Pencil, with white, blue and red wash,
> 37 × 24 cm
> Inscr. in Fuseli's hand bottom left:
> 'P[urser's] C[ross]. July, 07'
> Lit: Federmann 1927, pl.62 top; Sitwell 1943,
> p.216; Todd 1946, pl.20; Wilenski 1946,
> pp.167f., 223, 234, repr. 83; Levy 1966, p.202,
> repr. 129; Tomory 1972, repr. 208
> Schiff: 1444
> *London, Tate Gallery*, Inv. No.3396
> (formerly Sir Charles and Lady Holroyd)

Mrs Marion Grayson of Columbia University has suggested that this drawing might be an illustration of the scene in Samuel Richardson's *Pamela* where Mrs Jewkes presents Pamela to the cook and maid servant at breakfast. (cf. Samuel Richardson, *Pamela*, with an introduction by William M. Sale Jr., paperback edition, W.W. Norton, N 166, New York 1968, p.112.)

192 Two Female Heads [1810–1815]

> Pencil, 23.3 × 18.3 cm
> Schiff: 1672
> *Zurich, Kunsthaus*, Inv. No.1940/65

The top head has a hairstyle combining a plait and curls, decorated with flowers and a veil. The lower one has a short style with a bow and curls combed over the forehead.

On the same sheet, a quotation from G.B. Armenini, *De' veri precetti della pittura*, II, Ravenna 1587, p.99 (Leonardo's criticism of Michelangelo's 'Last Judgement' – that he had used too few models for such a large number of figures), as well as verses 193–7 of Euripides' *Phaedra*.

193 Woman with a Stiletto; Man's Head with a Startled Expression [1810–20]

> Pencil and black chalk, 20.1 × 14.5 cm
> Inscr. at top by an unknown hand: 'Mary Anne', 'Mary Anne Lamb'; and under the man's head, 'Fuseli'; on the back, also by an unknown hand: 'Nothing could afflict Mr F.'
> Lit: Schiff 1959, p.45; Powell 1959, p.359, repr. 64; Tomory 1972, repr. 56, p.127
> Schiff: 1615
> *Oxford, Visitors of the Ashmolean Museum*

The inscription seems to suggest that the disturbed young woman, whose right hand is depicted in three different positions holding a stiletto, is Mary Anne Lamb, the sister of the writer Charles Lamb, who in 1796 killed her mother in a fit of madness. In her left hand she is probably holding a piece of the foreleg of a young buck; in various other works by Fuseli Maenads are shown holding limbs of the same animal. On her head she wears a decoration resembling a bunch of grapes. Fuseli appears to associate murderesses with maenads or bacchantes,

194 Half-length Figures of Two Promenading Women, Turning towards Each Other in Conversation 1816

194

Pencil, 31.7 × 20 cm
Inscr. bottom right: 'M.G. [Margate] Sept. 16';
collection stamp of the Countess of Guilford;
On the back: 'Lady Macbeth Sleepwalking,
with the Doctor and Maid-servant', pencil with
some ink and grey wash; inscr. bottom right:
'M.G. [Margate] 5. Sept.' 17.'
Exh: Zurich 1926 (313); 1941 (412); 1969 (307)
Lit: Antal 1956, pl.40a, p.102
Schiff: 1682
Zurich, Kunsthaus, Inv. No.1926/367

In this composition Fuseli refers to the figures of
Hero and Ursula in his illustration to Shakespeare's
Much Ado About Nothing, III, 1, *Chalmer's Shake-
speare,* Vol.2, London 1805 (Schiff 1266).

195 Kneeling Woman Seen from the Back 1817

195

Based on the kneeling woman in
Raphael's 'Transfiguration'

Black chalk, 23.1 × 19.5 cm
Inscr. bottom right: 'P.H. [Putney Hill]
Oct. 3. 17'
Exh: Zurich 1926 (318); 1941 (423); 1969 (290)
Schiff: 1576
Zurich, Kunsthaus, Inv. No.1938/718
(Ganz Bequest)

196 Bust of a Woman with an Eccentric Coiffure 1818

Pencil and chalk, 18.7 × 11.2 cm
Inscr. bottom right: 'R.G. [Ramsgate]
12 Sept.' 18'
Schiff: 1685
Basle, Öffentliche Kunstsammlung,
Inv. No.1914.290

The coiffure consists of a high fringe of ringlets com-
ing down to her eyebrows and a large knot of hair
piled up high, twisted round several times and fastened with a comb.

197 Woman with an Eccentric Hairstyle 1821

196

Pencil, 13.4 × 18.6 cm
Inscr. top right: παιδολετειρα
June 4 21. P.H. [Putney Hill]'
Schiff: 1603
Oxford, Michael Maclagan

The woman has a hairpin between her teeth; in her
hands she holds a child's body, only sketchily outlined. The Greek inscription 'παιδολετειρα', or child
murderess (a name given to Medea in Greek literature), indicates that this drawing belongs to that
group of works in which Fuseli depicted courtesans
maiming or killing male infants or small boys.

197

198 A Seated Woman with an Extremely Eccentric Hairstyle, Turning away from the Spectator, a Book in her Left Hand 1822

Pencil and wash, 22.5 × 18.4 cm
Inscr. on her shoulder band, 'MAI XXII
P.H. [Putney Hill]'
On back, pencil sketch of a reclining woman
Exh: Zurich 1941 (431); 1969 (291)
Lit: Antal 1956, p.119, pl.62
Schiff: 1578
Zurich, Kunsthaus, Inv. No.1940/58

199 Study from the Life Class at the Royal Academy (I) 1800

Pen and ink over pencil with blue and grey wash, 18.2 × 15.5 cm
Inscr. bottom right: 'Acc. Nov. 1800'
On the reverse another model in the same pose; inscr. 'Acc.'
Schiff: 1454
Basle, Öffentliche Kunstsammlung,
Inv. No.1934.146

198

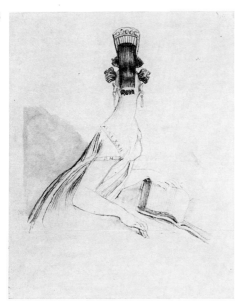

200 Study from the Life Class at the Royal Academy (II) 1801

Pen and ink with grey and blue wash,
18.4 × 14.5 cm
Inscr. in his own hand bottom right:
'Acc.Nov.1801'
Lit: Dörries 1943, p.85
Schiff: 1455
London, Trustees of the British Museum
Inv. No.1902-4-14-2

201 Cliff Caves near Margate 1792

Pencil, 23 × 18.5 cm
Inscr. bottom right: 'Margate Sept. 92'
Exh: Zurich 1926 (204); 1941 (304); London
1950 (76); New York 1954 (42); Bremen/
Dusseldorf 1957 (86); Zurich 1969 (227)
Lit: Ganz 1947, 48; Lankheit 1951, p.175;
Hofmann 1952, pp.166, 169
Schiff: 1187
Zurich, Kunsthaus, Inv. No.1938/758
(Ganz Bequest)

199

202 Steep Slopes near Devils Dyke, Sussex, with a View of the Sea [*c*.1790]

Pencil, 32 × 19.7 cm
Inscr. bottom right: 'Devils Dyke'
On the reverse a male nude seen from the back;
collection stamp of the Countess of Guilford
Exh: Zurich 1926 (339); 1941 (305); London
1950 (74); Zurich 1969 (229)
Lit: Ganz 1947, 47; Lankheit 1951, p.175;
Hofmann 1952, p.166
Schiff: 1189
Basle, Öffentliche Kunstsammlung,
Inv. No.1914-132-25

200

203

201

204

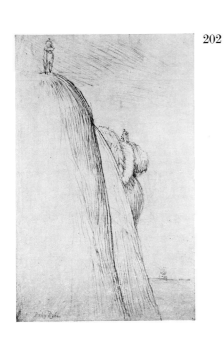

202

205

206

207

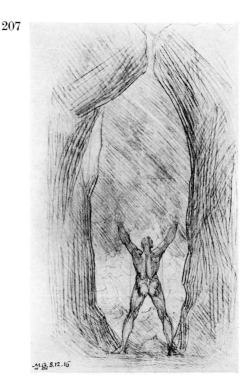

203 A Bearded Man Lifting a Stone above his Head
[c.1790]

Pen and sepia ink over pencil,
33.4 × 22.1 cm
At bottom right in pencil a small crouching
figure lifting a stone; on the back the collection
stamp of the Countess of Guilford
Exh: Zurich 1926 (186); 1941 (311); London
1950 (77); Bremen/Dusseldorf 1957 (83);
Zurich 1969 (224)
Lit: Federmann 1927, pl. opp. p.120, p.65;
Schrade 1931, p.15, note 29; Beutler 1939,
p.18, with repr.; Ganz 1947, text repr. p.41
Schiff: 1144
Basle, Öffentliche Kunstsammlung, Inv.
No.1914/132.1

Ferdinand Hodler is reputed to have asked, on being
shown this sheet, 'Who is it who is drawing like
myself?'.

204 Girl at a Window Overlooking the Sea 1821

Pencil, 14.9 × 11.7 cm
Inscr. top right: 'Bⁿ Septʳ 11. 21'
Schiff: 1572
Basle, Offentliche Kunstsammlung,
Inv. No.1933.224

205 A Man Asleep on the Sea Shore under a Bush
[1790–95]

Pen and sepia ink, 19.9 × 32.1 cm
Schiff: 1185
Hamburg, Kunsthalle (from the Kaesbach
Collection, Erfurt)

206 Cliffs on the South Coast of England [c.1790]

Pen and ink, 25.2 × 20.3 cm
On the reverse a sketch of three women
climbing down a dune
Exh: Zurich 1969 (226)
Lit: Ganz 1947, 46; Lankheit 1951, p.175;
Hofmann 1952, p.166
Schiff: 1186
Zurich, Kunsthaus, Inv. No.1938/641
(Ganz Bequest)

A couple are visible on the cliffs, the woman's shawl
is billowing in the wind.

**207 Sea Cave near Margate with a Nude Man seen
from the Back 1816**

Black chalk, 29.8 × 18.4 cm
Inscr. bottom left in sepia: 'M.G: S. 12. 16'
Schiff: 1726
Saffron Walden, Walter A. Brandt

Exhibitions

(Wartmann, Wilhelm), *Drawings by Henry Fuseli*, Kunsthaus Zurich, April-May 1913.

(Wartmann, Wilhelm), *Johann Heinrich Füssli – Henry Fuseli (1741-1825)*, paintings, drawings and engravings, Kunsthaus Zurich, 18 July–5 September 1926.

Paintings and Drawings by Henry Fuseli, R. E. A. Wilson, 24 Ryder Street, London S.W.1, March–April 1935.

(Wartmann, Wilhelm and Fischer, Marcel), *Johann Heinrich Füssli (1741–1825) Second Centenary Exhibition 1941*, Kunsthaus Zurich, 1941.

(Powell, Nicolas), *An Exhibition of Paintings and Drawings by Fuseli*, London, The Arts Council, 1950.

Paintings and Drawings by Fuseli, Roland, Browse & Delbanco, London 1948.

Liotard-Füssli, Paris/Geneva, 1948.

Fuseli Drawings, loan exhibition organized by the Pro Helvetia Foundation and circulated by the Smithsonian Institution, New York, 1954.

Johann Heinrich Füssli, organized by the Pro Helvetia Foundation, Bremen/Düsseldorf, 1957.

(Tomory, P. A.), *A Collection of Drawings by Henry Fuseli R. A.*, Auckland City Art Gallery, 1967; and London, Roland, Browse & Delbanco, 1968.

(Gert Schiff) *Johann Heinrich Füssli (1741–1825), Paintings and Drawings*, Kunsthaus Zurich, 17 May–6 July 1969.

Bibliography

Allentuck, Marcia, 'Fuseli's Nightmare', in *Woman as Sex Object*, ed. Thomas B. Hess and Linda Nochlin, New York 1973.

Anonymous, *Journal für Literatur und Kunst*; Vol.I, Zürich (Füssli und Compagnie); No.3; Vol.IX: 'Kunstanzeige: Ankündigung von Heinrich Füssli's Sämtlichen Werken; No.4: 'Ankündigung einer Folge von Kupferstichen aus Shakespeare, Milton und Dante, nach Gemälden von Heinrich Füssli Esq., gestochen von Moses Haughton' (sic, translated from English).

'Johann Heinrich Füssli' (Obituary), in *Kunstblatt*, No.28, Berlin, 6 April 1826.

Antal, Frederick, 'Fuseli Studies' (Reviews of two books – Eudo C. Mason, *The Mind of Henry Fuseli* and Nicolas Powell, *The Drawings of Henry Fuseli*, in Burlington Magazine XCVI, August 1954.

Antal, Frederick, *Fuseli Studies*, London 1956.

Antal, Frederick, *Hogarth and his Place in European Art*, London 1962.

Beutler, Ernst Rudolf, *Johann Heinrich Füssli; Ansprache bei Eröffnung der Füssli-Ausstellung des Frankfurter Goethe-Museums, 27 August 1938*, Halle an der Saale 1939.

Beutler, Ernst, *Führer durch das Frankfurter Goethe-Museum*, Frankfurt 1955.

Biermann, Georg, 'Die Neuerwerbungen für die königl. Nationalgalerie – Zur Ausstellung in der Akademie der Künste in Berlin', in *Der Cicerone*, Vol.III. No.19, Leipzig, October 1911.

Blunt, Anthony, *The Art of William Blake*, New York 1959.

Boase, T. S. R., *English Art 1800–1870*, Oxford, at the Clarendon Press, 1959.

Boase, T. S. R., 'Macklin and Bowyer', in *Journal of the Warburg and Courtauld Institutes*, XXVI, 1963.

Boydell, John, *A Catalogue of the Pictures etc. in the Shakespeare Gallery . .*, London 1790. Reissued London 1791, 1792, 1793, 1802.

Boydell, John and Boydell, Josiah, *A Collection of Prints, from Pictures Painted for the Purpose of Illustrating the Dramatic Works of Shakespeare, by the Artists of Great Britain*, London 1803 (foreword dated 1805).

Brion, Marcel, *Romantic Art*, London 1960.

Collins Baker, C. H., and James, Montague Rhodes, *British Painting*, Boston 1933.

Cunningham, Allan, 'Henry Fuseli', in *The Lives of the Most Eminent British Painters, Sculptors and Architects*, II, London 1830.

Cunningham, Allan, 'Introduction, Historical and Critical', in Pilkington, Matthew, A. M., *A General Dictionary of Painters*, London 1857.

Dafforne, James, 'British Artists: their Style and Character, with engraved illustrations, No.LVII – Henry Fuseli, R. A.', in *The Art Journal*, New Series, VII, 1861.

Dayes, Edward, 'Professional Sketches of Modern Artists, Fuseli, Henry, R. A.', in *The Works of the Late Edward Dayes*, London 1805.

Denk, Ferdinand, 'Goethe und die Bildkunst des Sturms und Drangs', in *Deutsche Vierteljahrsschrift für Literaturwissenschaft und Geistesgeschichte*, VIII, 1930.

Deonna, Waldemar, 'L'art suisse des origines à nos jours' in *Pro Arte et Libris*, Geneva, July–August 1943.

Ditchburn-Bosch, Ursula, 'Johann Heinrich Füsslis Kunstlehre und Ihre Auswirkung auf seine Shakespeare-Interpretation', dissertation, Zurich 1960.

Dörries, Bernhard, *Deutsche Zeichnungen des 18. Jahrhunderts*, Munich, 1943.

Dotson, Esther Gordon, 'English Shakespeare Illustrations and Eugene Delacroix', in *Essays in Honor of Walter Friedlaender*, New York University, Institute of Fine Arts, 1965.

Erffa, Helmut von, 'An Unidentified Subject by Fuseli Identified' in *Burlington Magazine*, LXXXXIX, April 1947.

Federmann, Arnold, *Johann Heinrich Füssli: Dichter und Maler 1741–1825*, Zürich/Leipzig 1927.

Fischer, Marcel, 'Das römische Skizzenbuch von Johann Heinrich Füssli (1741–1825)', in *Neujahrsblatt der Zürcher Kungstgesellschaft*, Zurich 1942.

Focillon, Henri, 'La peinture au XIXᵉ Siècle: Le Retour à L'Antique – Le Romantisme', *Manuels d'Histoire de l'Art*, Vol.X, ed. Henri Marcel, Paris 1927.

Forster, Johann Georg Adam, 'Geschichte der Kunst in England: Vom Jahre 1789', in *Georg Forsters Werke: Sämtliche Schriften, Tagebücher, Briefe*, ed. Gerhard Steiner, Vol.VII, Berlin 1963.

H. H. F. (Hans Heinrich Füssli), 'Heinrich Füssl der Jüngere', in *Allgemeines Künstlerlexikon*, ed. Johann Rudolf Füssli, Zurich 1806.

Füssli, Willhelm, *Zürich und die wichtigsten Städte am Rhein*, 2 Vols. Zurich/Winterthur 1842.

Ganz, Paul, *Die Zeichnungen Hans Heinrich Füsslis* (Henry Fuseli), Bern/Olten 1947.

Gaunt, William, *A Concise History of English Painting*, New York 1964.

Gradmann, Erwin and Cetto, Anna Maria, *Schweizer Malerei und Zeichnung im 17. und 18. Jahrhundert*, Basle 1944.

Grigson, Geoffrey, 'Painters of the Abyss!', in *The Architectural Review*, CVIII, Boston, Mass., October 1950.

Gurlitt, Cornelius, *Die deutsche Kunst des neunzehnten Jahrhunderts*, Berlin 1900.

Harcourt-Smith, Simon, 'Fuseli', in *Apollo*, LI, 1950 (Commentary on the Fuseli exhibition, London 1950).

Haydon, Benjamin Robert, and Hazlitt, William, 'Painting – The British School', in *Painting and the Fine Arts: Being the Articles under those Heads contributed to the Encyclopedia Britannica*, Edinburgh 1838.

Haydon, Benjamin Robert, *Life of Benjamin Robert Haydon, Historical Painter, from his Autobiography and Journals*, edited and compiled by Tom Taylor, Second Edition, 3 Vols. London 1853.

Haydon, Benjamin Robert, *The Diary of Benjamin Robert Haydon*, ed. Willard Bissell Pope, Harvard University Press, Cambridge, Mass., Vol.I and II 1960, III to V 1963.

Heffels, Monika, 'Die Handzeichnungen des 18. Jahrhunderts', in *Katalog des Germanischen Nationalmuseums Nürnberg, Die Deutschen Handzeichnungen*, Vol.IV, Nuremberg 1969.

Hofmann, Werner, 'Zu Füsslis geschichtlicher Stellung', in *Zeitschrift für Kungstgeschichte*, XV, 1952.

Hofstätter, Hans H., *Symbolismus und die Kunst der Jahrhundertwende: Voraussetzungen, Erscheinungsformen, Bedeutungen*, Cologne 1965.

Horner, Johann Jakob, 'Leben Johann Heinrich Füsslis von Zürich', *XXII Neujahrsstück der Künstlergesellschaft*, Zurich 1826.

Huber, Michel, *Catalogue raisonné du Cabinet d'estampes du feu M. Winckler.., I*, Leipzig 1802.

Irwin, David, 'Fuseli's Milton Gallery: Unpublished Letters' in *Burlington Magazine*, CI, 681, December 1959.

Irwin, David, *English Neoclassical Art: Studies in Inspiration and Taste*, London 1966.

Jaloux, Edmond, *Johann-Heinrich Füssli*, Montreux 1942.

Janson, Horst W., 'Fuseli's Nightmare', in *Arts and Sciences*, II, Spring 1963, I.

Josephson, Ragnar, *Sergels fantasi*, 2 Vols., Stockholm 1956.

Kaesbach-Kurella 'Aphorismen von H. Füssli', translated by Marie Kurella, with photographs by Dr Walter Kaesbach, *Zeitschrift für bildende Kunst*, 56, Vol.32, No.1, January 1921.

Kalman, Harold D., 'Füssli, Pope and the Nightmare', in *Pantheon*, XXIX, No.3, May–June 1971.

Kayser, Wolfgang, *Das Groteske: Seine Gestaltung in Malerei und Dichtung*, Oldenburg/Hamburg 1957.

Keller, Heinz, 'J. H. Füssli: Titania, von Oberon geweckt', in *Hauptwerke des Kunstmuseums Winterthur*, Winterthur 1948.

Keynes, Geoffrey, *Engravings by William Blake, The Separate Plates*, Dublin 1956.

Klingender, Francis D., *Art and the Industrial Revolution*, new publication by Arthur Elton, London 1968.

Knowles, John, *The Life and Writings of Henry Fuseli*, 3 Vols., London 1831.

Laban, Ferdinand, 'Die Zeichnungen auf der deutschen Jahrhundert-Austellung', in *Die graphischen Künste*, XXX, Vienna 1907.

La Farge, Henry A., 'Fuseli and Early Romantics', in *Art News*, II, January 1953; review of the exhibition *Romanticism in Eighteenth Century England*, New York, Durlacher Brothers, January 1953.

Lankheit, Klaus, 'Zur Füssli-Forschung, Gedanken im Anschluss an: Paul Ganz, Die Zeichnungen Hans Heinrich Füsslis', in *Zeitschrift für Kunstgeschichte*, XIV, 1951.

Leslie, Charles Robert, *A Handbook for Young Painters*, London 1854.

Levey, Michael, *From Giotto to Cézanne*, London 1963.

Levey, Michael, *Rococo to Revolution: Major Trends in Eighteenth-century Painting*, London 1966.

Macandrew, Hugh H., 'Henry Fuseli and William Roscoe', in *The Liverpool Libraries, Museums and Arts Committee Bulletin*, Vol.8, (Walker Art Gallery Number), Liverpool 1959–1960.

Macandrew, Hugh H., 'Selected Letters from the Correspondence of Henry Fuseli and William Roscoe of Liverpool', in *Gazette des Beaux-Arts*, LXII, October 1963.

Mandach, Conrad von, *Bericht über die Tätigkeit der Eidgenössischen Kommission der Gottfried Keller-Stiftung, 1932–1945*, Zurich 1946.

Mason, Eudo C., *The Mind of Henry Fuseli; Selections from his Writings with an Introductory Study*, London 1951.

Mason, Eudo C. (Ed.), 'Unveröffentlichte Gedichte von Johann Heinrich Füssli', in *Neujahrsblatt der Zürcher Kunstgesellschaft*, Zurich 1951.

Füssli, Johann Heinrich, *Remarks on the Writings and Conduct of J. J. Rousseau – Bemerkungen über J. J. Rousseaus Schriften und Verhalten*, ed. with introduction, translation and commentary by Eudo C. Mason, Zurich 1962.

Mason, Eudo C., 'Johann Heinrich Füssli und Shakespeare', in *Shakespeare und die Schweiz, Schweizer Theaterjahrbuch XXX der Schweizerischen Gesellschaft für Theaterkultur*, Berne 1964.

Merchant, W. Moelwyn, *Shakespeare and the Artist*, London, Oxford University Press 1959.

Meyer, Johann Heinrich, 'Entwurf einer Kungstgeschichte des 18. Jahrhunderts', in *Winckelmann und sein Jahrhundert: In Briefen und Aufsätzen*, ed. Johann Wolfgang von Goethe, Tubingen 1805.

Michel, Wilhelm, *Das Teuflische und Groteske in der Kunst*, ed. Munich 1919.

Middeldorf, Ulrich, 'An Exhibition of English Prints and Drawings at Chicago' in *Burlington Magazine*, LXXXVIII, December 1946.

Monk, Samuel H., *The Sublime: A Study of Critical Theories in XVIIIth Century England*, Ann Arbor, University of Michigan Press 1960 (first published in New York 1935).

Muther, Richard, *Geschichte der englischen Malerei*, Berlin 1903.

Oppel, Horst, *Die Shakespeare-Illustration als Interpretation der Dichtung*, Abhandlungen der Geistes-und sozialwissenschaftlichen Klasse 1965, No. 2. Akademie der Wissenschaften und der Literatur, Mainz.

Pauli, Gustav, 'Die Kunst des Klassizismus und der Romantik', in *Propyläen-Kungstgeschichte*, XIV, Berlin 1925.

Photiades, Vassily, *Eighteenth-century Painting*, translated from the French by Frances Partridge, New York 1964.

Powell, Nicolas, *The Drawings of Henry Fuseli*, London 1951.

Powell, C. N. P., 'Gert Schiff: Zeichnungen von Johann Heinrich Füssli' in *Burlington Magazine*, CI, September-October 1959.

Praz, Mario, 'Fuseli', in *La casa della fama*, Milan/Naples 1952.

Redgrave, Richard and Samuel, *A Century of British Painters*, ed. Ruthven Todd, London 1947.

Richardson, E. P., 'Fuseli's "Nightmare" ', in *Detroit Institute of Art Bulletin*, Vol.34, No.1, 1954-5.

Rosenblum, Robert, *Transformations in Late Eighteenth Century Art*, Princeton University Press 1960.

Salaman, Malcolm C., and Holme, Charles, 'Shakespeare in Pictorial Art', in *The Studio*, Spring 1916.

Sandby, William, *The History of the Royal Academy of Arts from its Foundation in 1768 to the Present Time*, 2 Vols., London 1862.

Saxl, Fritz, and Wittkower, Rudolf, *British Art and the Mediterranean*, London 1947.

Schiff, Gert, *Zeichnungen von Johann Heinrich Füssli (1741–1825)*, Schweizerisches Institut für Kunstwissenschaft, Kleine Schriften No.2, Zurich 1959.

Schiff, Gert, 'Füssli, Puritain et Satanique', in *L'Oeil*, LXIII, March 1960.

Schiff, Gert, 'Frederick Antal: Fuseli Studies', review in *Zeitschrift für Kunstgeschichte* 23, 1, 1960.

Schiff, Gert, *Johann Heinrich Füssli: Ein Sommernachtstraum*, Stuttgart 1961.

Schiff, Gert, *Johann Heinrich Füsslis Milton-Galerie*, Schweizerisches Institut für Kunstwissenschaft, No.4, Zurich/Stuttgart 1963.

Schiff, Gert, *Johann Heinrich Füssli und Michelangelo*, Schweizerisches Institut für Kunstwissenschaft, Annual Report, Zurich 1964.

Schiff, Gert, 'Johann Heinrich Füssli in Zürich', in *Librarium*, Journal of the Schweizerische Bibliophilen-Gesellschaft, 7, No.2, Zurich, August 1964, re-published in catalogue *Johann Heinrich Füssli – 1741–1825, Gemälde und Zeichnungen*, Kunsthaus, Zurich, 17 May–6 July 1969.

Schiff, Gert, *Echtheits-und Zuschreibungsprobleme bei Johann Heinrich Füssli*, Schweizerisches Institut für Kunstwissenschaft, Annual Report, Zurich 1965.

Schmid, Max, *Kunstgeschichte des XIX, Jahrhunderts*, I, Leipzig 1904.

Schneck, Jerome, M. D., 'Henry Fuseli: Nightmare, and Sleep Paralysis', in *The Journal of the American Medical Association*, Vol.207, No.427, Chicago, January 1969.

Schrade, Hubert, 'Die romantische Idee von der Landschaft als höchstem Gegenstand christlicher Kunst', in *Neue Heidelberger Jahrbücher*, Heidelberg 1931.

Schrade, Hubert, 'Franz Landsberger, Die Kunst der Goethezeit', review in *Kritische Berichte zur kunstgeschichtlichen Literatur*, Leipzig/Zurich 1931–1932, No.1.

Sitwell, Sacheverell, *Narrative Pictures: A Survey of English Genre and its Painters*, London 1937.

Sitwell, Sacheverell, *Splendours and Miseries*, London 1943.

Solier, René de, *L'Art fantastique*, Paris 1961.

Stengel, Walter, *Erster Bericht über die Neuerwerbungen des Kupferstichkabinetts, Pfingsten 1911–1913*, Nuremberg 1913.

Thornbury, G. Walter, 'Fuseli at Somerset House', in *The Art Journal*, New Series VI, 1860.

Timbs, John, *Anecdote Biography, William Hogarth, Sir Joshua Reynolds, Thomas Gainsborough, Henry Fuseli, Sir Thomas Lawrence and J. M. W. Turner*, London, 1860.

Todd, Ruthven, 'The Reputation and Prejudices of Henry Fuseli', in *Tracks in the Snow*, London 1946.

Tomory, P. A., *A Collection of Drawings by Henry Fuseli R. A.*, Auckland City Art Gallery, 1967.

Tomory, Peter, *The Life and Art of Henry Fuseli*, London 1972.

Weinberger, Martin, *Deutsche Rokokozeichnungen*, Munich 1923.

Wilenski, R. H., *An Outline of English Painting*, London 1946.

Winner, Matthias, 'Gert Schiff: Johann Heinrich Füsslis Milton Galerie', review in *Zeitschrift für Kunstgeschichte*, Vol.28, 1965.

Woodward, John, 'Paintings and Drawings by Fuseli', in *Burlington Magazine*, XCII, April 1950.

Young, John, *A Catalogue of the Celebrated Collection of Pictures of the Late John Julius Angerstein, Esq.*, London 1823.

Lenders